M000286246

EXPERIENCING THE
HEAVENLY REALM

Experiencing the Heavenly Realm

Keys to Accessing Supernatural Experiences

Judy Franklin

WITH CONTRIBUTIONS BY BENI JOHNSON

© Copyright 2011 – Judy Franklin and Beni Johnson

All rights reserved. This book is protected by the copyright laws of the United States of America. This book may not be copied or reprinted for commercial gain or profit. The use of short quotations or occasional page copying for personal or group study is permitted and encouraged. Permission will be granted upon request. Unless otherwise identified, Scripture quotations are taken from the NEW AMERICAN STANDARD BIBLE', Copyright © 1 960,1962,1963,1968,1971,1972,1973,1975,1977,1995 by The Lockman Foundation. Used by permission. Scripture quotations marked NKJV are taken from the New King James Version. Copyright © 1982 by Thomas Nelson, Inc. Used by permission. All rights reserved. Scripture quotations marked KJV are taken from the King James Version. Please note that Destiny Image's publishing style capitalizes certain pronouns in Scripture that refer to the Father, Son, and Holy Spirit, and may differ from some publishers' styles. Take note that the name satan and related names are not capitalized. We choose not to acknowledge him, even to the point of violating grammatical rules. Bold emphasized text within Scripture is the author's own.

Some quotes attributed to Bill Johnson of Bethel Church, Redding, California, come from his spoken messages and are used with his permission.

DESTINY IMAGE. PUBLISHERS, INC.
P.O. Box 310, Shippensburg, PA 17257-0310
"Speaking to the Purposes of God for This Generation and for the Generations to Come."

This book and all other Destiny Image, Revival Press, MercyPlace, Fresh Bread, Destiny Image Fiction, and Treasure House books are available at Christian bookstores and distributors worldwide.

For a U.S. bookstore nearest you, call 1-800-722-6774.
For more information on foreign distributors, call 717-532-3040.
Reach us on the Internet: www.destinyimage.com.

ISBN 13 TP: 978-0-7684-3651-8
ISBN 13 HC: 978-0-7684-3652-5
ISBN 13 LP: 978-0-7684-3653-2
ISBN 13 Ebook: 978-0-7684-9037-4

For Worldwide Distribution, Printed in the U.S.A.

1 2 3 4 5 6 7 8 9 10 11 / 14 13 12 11

DEDICATION

I dedicate this book to my children and their spouses, Jonathan, Daniel and Greta, and Susanna and Jay; to my grandchildren, Kendra, Jesse, Erik, Elyas, Asher, Jordan and Tobin; and to my great-grandson, Harlan. I want your floor to be my ceiling. I want your inheritance from me to be a head start in walking farther with God than I could ever go. I pray this book will spur each of you on to greater depths with the most wonderful God of all eternity.

I love you all very much!

Mom and Grandma Juju

ACKNOWLEDGMENTS

Bill and Beni Johnson ~ You both are the most amazing people. You have raised me to love God more, you have taught me what grace is, and you have only shown grace to me. I would not be where I am or who I am without your love and support. Thank you.

Beni ~ Thank you so much for your willingness to write the opening and closing chapters for this book.

Kris Vallotton ~ I have learned so much from you. Thank you for helping to shape my life. You are amazing.

Randall Worley ~ While God gave me my wings, you continue to add feathers to them so I can soar higher. Thank you.

Bob Jones ~ You have imparted to me over and over again. It was you who inspired me to keep on going higher. Thank you.

Vanessa Chandler, Dianne Brown, Julia Loren, Allison Armerding, and Pam Spinosi ~ Thank you for your input into this book.

Banning Liebscher ~ Thank you for your word about me making this a "how to" book and not one just about my experiences.

Dann Farrelly ~ Your input was invaluable. Thank you so much.

To all of you who let me share your testimonies ~ Thank you.

Julie Winter ~ Honestly, without you this book would never have been finished. Your encouragement and friendship mean so much to me. Thank you for believing in this book even when I didn't.

ENDORSEMENTS

The great apostle Paul wrote to the Corinthians and said, *"Now concerning spiritual **gifts**, brethren, I do not want you to be unaware"* (1 Cor. 12:1). The word *gifts* is not in the Greek text because Paul was not just trying to teach us about spiritual gifts, he was explaining to us how the spirit world works.

The Church has lost access to the spirit realm in this postmodern age. We have exchanged the valuable for the visible and washed up on the shores of the logical, tangible, and predictable. The Church's inability to bring people into a true spiritual experience with the Father has created a vortex for every dark spirit to suck seekers into its clutches.

Judy Franklin has done a masterful job calling the Church back to her original mandate to live in the spirit realm. Her book *Experiencing the Heavenly Realm* reads like a treasure map, taking us on a journey from the house of horrors to supernatural experiences. Judy hands us the lost keys to the mysterious Kingdom and shows us the way to the Father's house.

If you have been longing to pass through the veil into the hidden realms of Heaven, this book is for you!

Kris Vallotton
Senior Associate Leader, Bethel Church, Redding, CA
Co-Founder, Bethel School of Supernatural Ministry
Author of *The Supernatural Ways of Royalty* and *Purity, the New Moral Revolution*

My relationship with Judy Franklin now spans several years. In that period I have been enriched every time she shared with me the transcendent encounters that she has had with the Father. Mystics are often dismissed by those who are content to remain in their safe and shallow streams of spiritual understanding. They are deemed as pushing the envelope too much with their ethereal and perceived esoteric experiences. I have known Judy to be very careful and committed as she seeks scriptural verification from those she has esteemed to be students of Scripture. In this, her maiden voyage into the publishing arena, she invites all of us to ascend into the heavenly realm of revelation to breathe the fresh air of the Father's unconditional love. You will be taken far above the polluted atmosphere of near-sighted religious ideas. The transparency of her testimony and subsequent discoveries of the Father's indescribable compassion will cause you to hunger for more.

Randall Worley
Headwaters Ministries
Ft. Mill, SC

Experiencing the Heavenly Realm is a timely book written out of Judy Franklin's rich experience in God. It is full of revelation that is uncomplicated yet deeply rooted in godly wisdom. Most importantly, this book reflects the hunger of a woman with a passion to experience all that Heaven has to offer. After reading the manuscript, I was reminded of the Father's heart for humanity and His desire for us to see into the heavenly realm. Caution! This book is highly contagious with the love of God and could be dangerous to casual Christianity.

Larry Randolph
Larry Randolph Ministries
Franklin, TN
Author of *User Friendly Prophecy* and *The Coming Shift*

If you're anything like me, this visionary book will stir you to repair your tent of meeting and look even more intently into the brilliant face of Abba, Father. I highly commend this work; it is packed with the kind of wisdom and revelation that only comes from personal encounter.

Dr. Mark Stibbe
Founder and Leader, The Father's House Trust, Watford, UK

We live in the greatest outpouring the world has ever seen. Without question, God is moving in the earth and stirring His Church to greater depths in the knowledge of Him. In the midst of this outpouring God is raising up voices to equip, encourage, and call His children into deeper realms of intimacy with Him. Judy Franklin is one of those voices. She writes with not only the revelation of Heaven but the authority of one who has experienced God in fresh and unique ways. I have personally seen the fruit of these experiences and the impact it has had on our community. Her story is not one written on the fringes of the Church but is established firmly in community as she pursues God. *Experiencing the Heavenly Realm* will inspire all who read it to give themselves fully to a God who is extravagantly in love with His children. My prayer is that you would not only read this book to learn about what is available, but that you would read this book to begin the journey of a lifetime that will lead you into the arms of the Father.

Banning Liebscher
Jesus Culture Director, Bethel Church
Redding, CA
Author of *Jesus Culture: Living a Life that Transforms the World*

Judy Franklin didn't just simply write a book...she wrote her life. While reading this book I could actually feel Heaven... Himself. I just sat back and smiled, shaking my head. "She did it," I said. She was able to capture Him and all of his goodness in word form. She captured my Friend. She captured Him and how fun He is. (Laughing...) Well done, Judy, my friend. Ya did Him proud; He smiles on this book. I love you so much.

Jenn Johnson
Worship Leader at Bethel Church
Brian and Jenn Johnson Ministries
Redding, CA

Judy Franklin's *Experiencing the Heavenly Realm* is a personal journey of spirit, discovering the reality of the presence of God, and literally hearing Him speak in great kindness. The encouragement to awaken our "spiritual eyes" and our "spiritual ears" is crucial to the intent of the book. Judy gets to tell her own story and at the same time leads the reader into his or her own journey of spirit-empowered imagination. The book is truly an experiential read, where the story and the teaching are juxtaposed as interwoven threads. Those readers only wanting information will be challenged by the experiential flow of thought designed to provoke imaginative engagement. Those only looking for experience (the obvious main aim of this book) will be also be provoked by its teaching content. You are invited into a journey of personal revelation.

David Crabtree
Senior Leader, DaySpring Church,
Castle Hill, NSW, Australia

"The surest way to speak a word of authority is to speak a word that you have been given personal insight on by experience in God. That sort of thing can never be taken from you. Nothing can diminish the effect of that word in your life. I can forget what I have learned to memorize. I can forget the key phrases and slogans, but I can never forget my experiences in God." —Bill Johnson

CONTENTS

FOREWORD

"A sated man loathes honey, but to a famished man any bitter thing is sweet" (Prov. 27:7). This verse, perhaps more than any other, describes why some enter into the realms of God more easily than others. When we are full and satisfied we become critics, while those who are desperate tend to rejoice in anything that is available. The actual capacity to discern diminishes with the lack of hunger. That is why so many experts missed Jesus when He came. They were satisfied with their religious system and lost the hunger for the greater things. But this is a new day.

I have never been more thrilled with what I see God doing in the Church than I am right now. While we have our challenges, the hunger that is truly a gift from God is at the highest point I've ever seen. And it is spreading worldwide.

Hunger produces people who will live with risk, believing in a big God and little devil. This hunger for the authentic Gospel, the kind preached and experienced in the Bible, is increasingly burning within the hearts of so many. And our perfect heavenly Father is ready to answer by *giving the Holy Spirit and not a stone* to those who ask. When hunger gets strong, people experience the things of God in new ways.

Judy Franklin and Beni Johnson have written a book that is very timely in that it answers part of the heart's cry of the people of God. Our hunger is for Him. But often we stop short of a God encounter because we are satisfied with good theology. Theology is wonderful. But it is not the same as the invitation from God to encounter Him in new and deeper ways. For example, the whole concept of being "seated in heavenly places in Christ" was never meant to be reduced to a doctrine (see Eph. 2:6). It was always meant to be an invitation from God to encounter Him and live from Heaven's perspective. But short of an experience, we can only imagine. Once again we fall short, as God is not an idea, a formula, or a ritual. He is a person to be known, and One with whom we interact.

These two authors are among the most qualified people I know for such an endeavor to write a book about experiencing God. One is my wife and the other is my secretary. And yes, I am biased. But I have watched as the life of fruitfulness needed for such a book has been lived in public and in private. The really fun part of this journey is to watch how their stories and experiences stir the hearts of people for more of what God has made available in our day. They are, in fact, introducing many of us to part of our inheritance in Christ:

an inheritance of encountering God and experiencing realms of Heaven now.

Their insights are rich with hope and full of promise. In reading this book, one cannot help but wonder how much more God will give us in this lifetime. It's as though they give us permission to pursue God, assuming nothing would be withheld from us if we asked. It's not too good to be true. *It's so good it is true.*

Pray, laugh, and sing, all while reading. *Experiencing the Heavenly Realm* is a journey you won't soon forget.

Bill Johnson
Pastor, Bethel Church, Redding, CA
Author of *When Heaven Invades Earth* and *Face to Face with God*

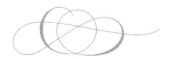

INTRODUCTION

Bill Johnson recently said, "One of the greatest needs in the Church right now is a revelation of Heaven. The reason being that God wants to entrust the resources of earth to a people who have their heart anchored in another world."

Throughout this book the "I" refers to the author, Judy Franklin. The exception being Chapters 1 and 28, which were written by Beni Johnson.

Heavenly experiences are what this book is about...a heart anchored in another world. Hopefully you will see how you can have a closer relationship with the Father, Son, and Holy Spirit. I will share some of my own heavenly experiences as well as stories of others. In addition, I will outline obstacles to seeing and show you how to have heavenly experiences for yourself.

As you read the stories about these experiences, my hope and prayer is for you to learn how to develop a more intimate relationship with the Lord on your own. Jesus so desires to have a deeper relationship with you. He wants you to know Him and know His ways, not just know *about* Him.

A relationship by definition is a connection, behavior, or feelings toward somebody else—friendship. That's the kind of relationship God wants with you. We can't know someone by just reading a book about him or her. To have a relationship we have to connect and interact with that person.

One day the Lord spoke to me. He simply said, "Ronald Reagan" (our president at the time). And that's all He said. I waited but He said nothing else.

So I said, "Yes, he's our president."

Then God said, "You can read about him every day."

"Yes, I can read about him in magazines and books," I replied.

He said, "You can hear about him every day."

Well of course, I thought, *I could hear about him on the television, radio, or even in conversations with people who are discussing him or what he's doing.*

He went on, "And you are affected by what he does."

"Oh yes, he signs bills and laws that do affect my life."

Then He asked, "How well do you know him?"

Wow! I was brought up short. I didn't know Ronald Reagan at all. I really only knew *about* him.

The Lord said, "You can read about Me every day."

I responded, "Yes, in the Bible and different books."

He said, "You can hear about Me every day."

And I said, "Yes, on the television, radio, and at church."

Then the Lord said, "You are affected by what I do."

"Oh yes." I knew where this was going.

Finally, the Lord asked, "How well do you know Me?"

I realized then that I knew *about* Him, but I didn't really know Him on a personal basis. He wants us to know Him.

> *No longer do I call you slaves, for the slave does not know what his master is doing; but I have called you friends, for all things that I have heard from My Father I have made known to you* (John 15:15).

The Lord has called us friends. Well, it takes more than reading, hearing, or being affected by what someone does to actually be a friend. The heavenly realm is open to a new level of friendship. It is a mystery. How can we be friends with the God of the universe, the God of eternity, the God of power and might? Jesus said:

> *...To you it has been granted to know the mysteries of the kingdom of God, but to the rest it is in parables,*

*so that SEEING THEY MAY NOT SEE, AND HEAR-
ING THEY MAY NOT UNDERSTAND* (Luke 8:10).

I don't want to be someone who just knows the *parables*. I want to know the *mysteries*. Don't you?

Out of this place of relationship come visions that connect our natural world to His spiritual realm. These visions release us not only into *pure* love but into a close connection with God.

These experiences with God will remove obstacles that keep us from receiving more of Him, learning more about Him, and becoming healed, whole, and intimate with Him. While you are experiencing His pure love you discover you've stepped onto the path of your destiny.

I once read a quote attributed to Deitrich Bonhoeffer, a German theologian who was executed by the Nazis in World War II: *"Truth divorced from experience must always dwell in the realm of doubt."* Think about that. Truth without an experience can create a niggle of doubt in your mind. You may know God is able and willing to heal people, because the Scriptures say so, and you've read that Jesus healed everyone who came to Him. Yet you may struggle with thoughts that God is not willing to heal because you have never seen or experienced healing for yourself or someone you've prayed for.

It's important that you have your own experiences with God. Our God is loving and kind and He wants an intimate relationship with us. Randall Worley once said, *"If God only wanted us to do things, then He would have made us angels. He wants a relationship with us."*

My prayer for you as you read the following pages is that you will find a path of knowing a loving and kind God who wants a relationship with you and wants you to soar like the eagle.

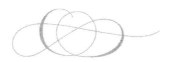

CHAPTER 1

Healing the Whole Man

by Beni Johnson

God's desire and design is to meet us, heal us, and love us. He will do anything He can to accomplish that meeting. He will spilt the heavens wide open for us to come to Him. He longs for us more than we long for Him. There is nothing more exciting than seeing a person connect to the heart of Heaven.

Years ago my husband and I were talking with a pastor. He was at the end of his rope so to speak, telling us he had tried everything to get answers and direction. He was tired and burned out and didn't know what else to do. We talked some more, and I finally looked at him and said, *"You need to soak!"* He looked at me and said, "Tell me about that." I told him he needed to lie on the floor, put a good worship CD on, and just lie there. I went on to tell him that he shouldn't ask or even talk to God, just soak in His presence and listen. He stared at me for a moment and said, "That's actually what I need." It was kind of fun to watch his face as he "got it." It made sense.

I feel strongly that God wants to connect with us more than we want to connect with Him. We need to stop and lay all the things that entangle us down and enter into His rest. And to top that off, when someone who is broken has a heavenly encounter, so much healing can take place in that moment.

Before Jesus ascended to Heaven to be at the right hand of the Father, He commissioned us.

> *...All authority has been given to Me in heaven and on earth. Go therefore and make disciples of all the nations, baptizing them in the name of the Father and of the Son and of the Holy Spirit, teaching them to observe all things that I have commanded you...* (Matthew 28:18-20 NKJV).

What are those "all things" in verse 20? Matthew 10:8 tells us that we are to *"heal* [cure] *the sick, raise the dead, cleanse the lepers, cast out demons."* So Jesus has been given authority, and He turns to us His disciples and tells us to go and do all the things that He was given authority to do.

When we look at Matthew 10:8 and read the part about healing the sick, many of us automatically think of physical healing. In the Greek language, the word *sick (as-then-eh'-o)* means "to be diseased, impotent, made weak or to be feeble in any sense." [1]

When I look at that verse, I see it saying *all* sickness—inside and out. God wants all men and women and children to be well from the inside out or the outside in. Anyone who is feeble in any sense, any person who is impotent, which is "deficient in capacity," can be healed.

You don't have to go very far to see that many are in a place of needing the healing presence that comes and heals the feebleness—that impotence that keeps us void of life and vigor. Many people come to us as Christians needing that encounter with God. They are so in need of having strength to get through a day. They come in brokenness looking for something to help them. Isn't it amazing that Jesus entrusted us to take His authority and release it onto others in need? To bring them into an encounter with the Most Holy One, to let them see how much God loves them?

I once did a mini-study on Isaiah 61:1-9 (NKJV), and I found some interesting things:

The Spirit of the Lord God is upon Me

Because the Lord has anointed Me

To preach good tidings to the poor;

He has sent Me to heal the brokenhearted,

To proclaim liberty to the captives,

And the opening of the prison to those who are bound;

To proclaim the acceptable year of the Lord,

And the day of vengeance of our God;

To comfort all who mourn,

To console those who mourn in Zion,

To give them beauty for ashes,

The oil of joy for mourning,

The garment of praise for the spirit of heaviness;

That they may be called trees of righteousness,

The planting of the Lord, that He may be glorified.

And they shall rebuild the old ruins,

They shall raise up the former desolations,

And they shall repair the ruined cities,

The desolations of many generations.

Strangers shall stand and feed your flocks,

And the sons of the foreigner

Shall be your plowmen and your vinedressers.

But you shall be named the priests of the Lord,

They shall call you the servants of our God.

You shall eat the riches of the Gentiles,

And in their glory you shall boast.

Instead of your shame you shall have double honor,

And instead of confusion they shall rejoice in their portion.

Therefore in their land they shall possess double;

Everlasting joy shall be theirs.

For I, the Lord, love justice;

I hate robbery for burnt offering;

I will direct their work in truth,

And will make with them an everlasting covenant.

Their descendants shall be known among the Gentiles,

And their offspring among the people.

All who see them shall acknowledge them,

That they are the posterity whom the Lord has blessed.

Several years back I had been doing some work with one of our pastors who helped people with very shattered pasts. Some of these people had been so shattered as small children that they had departmentalized their personalities out of a need for safety from abuse. They were truly shattered in their minds. We would pray and counsel with them and help them get to a place of safety so they could integrate back to a whole personality.

One day during this time I was reading this passage in Isaiah, which is a prophetic word concerning Jesus. I started looking up the meaning of some of the words. Verse 1 in NKJV says, "*heal the brokenhearted,*" which means "to bind up." I also found that the word *brokenhearted* means "shattered minds."[2] So this prophetic verse in Isaiah foretold Jesus coming to earth many years in the future with this as one of His assignments: to take those shattered in their minds and to bind them up as one would bind up a wound, to bring healing.

We also find in this passage that those who mourn are to be consoled and comforted and that they will be given beauty for their ashes, joy for their mourning, and a garment of praise for their heaviness.

Then in verse 3 we see a change. God gives these people their identity. Those who have been shattered now become trees of righteousness that God Himself will plant for His glory.

In verses 4-7 (NKJV), we see that God gives those who now have identity a destiny. Read this passage again:

And they shall rebuild the old ruins,

They shall raise up the former desolations,

And they shall repair the ruined cities,

The desolations of many generations.

Strangers shall stand and feed your flocks,

And the sons of the foreigner

Shall be your plowmen and your vinedressers.

But you shall be named the priests of the Lord,

They shall call you the servants of our God.

You shall eat the riches of the Gentiles,

And in their glory you shall boast.

Instead of your shame you shall have double honor,

And instead of confusion they shall rejoice in their portion.

Therefore in their land they shall possess double;

Everlasting joy shall be theirs.

Now we see how God has healed and restored, yet He has not only restored but also brought them into who they are and what they are to do.

The James Moffatt translation of the Bible says, *"They suffered shame in double measure, abuse and insult were their lot; so now in their own land they shall get double—theirs is a lasting joy"* (Isa. 61:7).

It's obvious what this passage is telling us: those who come out of brokenness can and will come into a great destiny. They will take those things, those places that have been ruined and in desolation for many generations and restore them. And, not only that, they will have lasting joy, everlasting joy!

It is like a huge dose of authority will be given to them. The devil tries to destroy us and keep us in our brokenness, and Jesus comes along and says, "Here, take Me. Let Me show you who you really are. Let Me show you your future."

I believe that when God sets you free from a disease of the body, soul, or spirit, you now have an authority to help others come into healing from that very thing you were delivered from.

Many years ago I was plagued with depression. Self-pity was my friend. I'm talking about the gut kind of depression that eats you up, the despair that attacks your inner being. When I was in my late teens, God delivered me from all depression in an instant. I will never forget that day. I was walking out of a bathroom and I cried out inside of me, "God, if You don't deliver me from this, I don't know what will happen to me." It wasn't that I was trying to boss God around; it was a very desperate cry for help. As I stepped through the door of the bathroom, I was set free. It lifted and has never returned after all these years. Now that's the way to get free! I wish it could be that way for all of us.

As I got older and matured in Christ, I found that an authority had been given to me to help others get free. When God comes and sets a person free, he or she is placed into his destiny. When you see people who are ravished, shattered, and broken come into freedom, it is a grace and a beauty to behold. Then that free person steps into his anointing and destiny, and you watch him take another broken person by the hand. There is compassion to see freedom come.

That's the way of Love, and that's the way of our Father.

I've written all that to say this:

There are many who are coming out of brokenness who will step into their destinies and will carry unique giftings and anointings. As with Judy, each of them will be very unique. And they need a place in the Body of Christ to use their gifts. They need leadership to pastor and keep them safe. I have watched so many be set free and—best of all—fall in love with the Trinity through the simple act of having a heavenly encounter. This is what Judy leads people into.

For all of us who come out of brokenness and are seeking true union with God, and not just with people, this realm of the heavenly is open to us. I believe that God loves to show us His realm and is longing for us to see and feel what it is like to be with Him. Why not begin to experience His heavenly realm while we wait for His return or our own homegoing?

Endnotes

1. "sick." *Strong's Concordance Greek Lexicon,* 772. Accessed 2010. http://www.eliyah.com/lexicon.html.

2. Brown, Driver, Briggs and Gesenius. "Hebrew Lexicon entry for Shabar." The KJV Old Testament Hebrew Lexicon. Accessed 2010. http://www.biblestudytools.com/lexicons/hebrew/kjv/shabar.html.

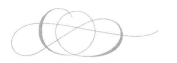

CHAPTER 2

PURE LOVE

Within God's presence, within His glory, a love exists that is seemingly incomprehensible. This love even goes beyond the love described in First Corinthians 13. It is the love we have forever imagined and hoped for. It is bigger, better, and greater than anything we could ever have thought possible. I felt it intensely one day during a Heaven-initiated encounter. I know that this love is for me...for you...for all people. No matter how evil or how good we are, He still loves us. His love is complete. He doesn't love one over the other. His heart beats with love. He truly is love. I know. I felt it, saw it, and breathed it.

Floored by Love

What does this love feel like? Let me tell you...it is beyond wonderful. The first time I felt this love was at my home church, Bethel Church in Redding, California. I had been called up on the platform to share about a God-encounter that I had experienced on a recent trip to Toronto Airport Christian Fellowship. I shared about seeing Jesus, and after I shared I honestly don't know what happened.

However, I suddenly found myself lying on the floor in front of the whole church. For some reason this struck me funny. Being new to this, I didn't know what I should do next. *Should I jump up quickly and act like nothing happened? Do I roll or crawl off the stage?* As the service went on I finally decided I would just sit up, and maybe Karen, who was sitting by me, would instruct me on what to do next. Well, I could not get up. It was as though I was glued to the floor. So then I thought, *I might as well lie here and listen to the rest of the service.* But God had another idea.

As I was lying there, I saw a vision of God's hand holding a rock. Then with His other hand God began knocking on the rock and it started to crack like an eggshell. As the pieces of rock fell away, I realized that in His hand He was holding a heart. The heart was dark and was barely moving. As He held the heart, the color returned and the heart began beating more strongly. He then said, "This is what I'm doing in the Body—the Church. I'm causing the hardness to fall away and am restoring health."

The Light

Then I looked up and saw the brightest, most beautiful light. I was in awe of its beauty. I said repeatedly to Karen,

"Look! It's so beautiful." The "light" kept coming closer to me, growing in size. I don't understand how, but I knew the light was God's glory, His very presence. Earlier I had been having encounters during prayer where I would see a large castle door opening, followed by a light coming through the doorway, covering me. This light felt wonderful and I was compelled to worship. I realized that this beautiful light represented God's presence, His glory. This light had visited me every day for three months and I hadn't known what it was.

As I lay on the platform the glory got so low that I could reach my hand out and touch it. Oh how soft, how wonderful it was. It kept coming down and it became so bright that I could hardly keep my eyes open. I put my hand over my eyes, peeking through my fingers until I finally had to keep my eyes shut or be blinded. Still it kept coming. I breathed it in with every breath I took. It filled my lungs and permeated my very being. The glory was heavy and it felt like I was being pushed down, even though I was on the floor.

Finally, I knew that I couldn't take this glory on my physical being anymore. I felt like I was going to die, but I wasn't afraid. In fact, I didn't even care. What a way to go! Very calmly I told Him, "Well, I'm going to die now." As I waited in His presence the glory started to withdraw. I didn't realize it at first, but I eventually found that I could open my eyes. I could still see the glory light and could wave my hand through it, but it was receding. I called out to Him, "Don't go, or if you go, take me with You." I didn't want to live without that presence—a presence that felt like pure love, the purest love that I had ever known, filling all of my senses.

By the time I was able to get up from the platform, the service was over. About a month later I was given the opportunity to share what had happened to me with our congregation.

CHAPTER 3

Too Stupid to Be Loved

You see, this was the first time in my life I had felt love. I thought that I was someone who just could not be loved, and as a result I had a hard time receiving any love. It may seem silly to you, but the circumstances in my life told me that it was true.

Painful Memories

I grew up knowing my dad did not want me. While other children had cute little nicknames, my nickname was "whang-brain." If I spilled my milk at dinner, which was probably often, my dinner was put on the kitchen floor. I was told I had to eat like a dog because I was sloppy, or I was put in the bathtub with my food. My dad liked my brother and preferred him over me. Whenever he had to take us somewhere, he would tell my brother to come with him and tell me to stay in the car. I knew he was ashamed of me, but I did not understand why.

I wrote Dear Abby once when I was about 9 years old and asked her why my dad didn't love me even though I tried to do what was right. The letter was never sent, but my mother found it and gave it to my dad. I can remember sitting on the end of my bed right by the door, listening closely, hoping he would say that he did love me after all. Instead, he bellowed that maybe he could love me if I wasn't so stupid. So that was the problem. I was stupid, and stupid people can't be loved.

It became clear when I was in the first grade that I was not as bright as the other children. But it wasn't until I was in the eighth grade that I was tested and found to have learning disabilities. I was then put in the "mentally retarded" class, as it was called at the time. Yes, I was stupid and this was why my dad was ashamed of me.

Unfortunately, I never really felt loved by my mother either. My mother was a broken person and was unable to protect me from the meanness of my father. One day, when I was 3 or 4 years old, my mother was painting the living room and accidentally left a cup of turpentine on the kitchen table. I awoke from a nap and went into the kitchen. Thinking the cup was filled with water, I drank it. I was rushed to the hospital and had my stomach pumped. After I returned home, my kidneys started to shut down. I found out much later that my mother called a doctor and begged him to come to the house. We didn't have very much money and she told him she would pay him a dime a month for the rest of her life, which was not easy in the early 1950s. He had compassion; he came and put me on antibiotics and again my life was saved. About the time I turned 14, my mother became a full-fledged alcoholic and physically, mentally, and emotionally wasn't there for anyone.

My dad's mother came to live with us sometime after the turpentine incident. I found out much later that my grandmother didn't like my mother and had tried to talk my dad into leaving her. One day while she was taking care of my brother and me, she took me on her lap. She told me that my mother had left the paint thinner out on purpose because I was no good. She said that I would never be any good, no matter how hard I tried, because my mother was evil.

So I grew up feeling unloved, stupid, and worthless. Years later, after I was married, my grandmother lay dying of cancer and she began to ask forgiveness from everyone she had hurt. Realizing she did not have much time, she became insistent that she had to see me. By the time the family asked me to come see her, she was comatose and unable to speak. I believe the reason that she so wanted to see me was because she wanted to ask for forgiveness, and I have forgiven her.

The Enemy's Lies

Of course we all do stupid things, but it was different for me. Whenever I did something stupid, I felt a constant reminder that I was unlovable. Even after I married and had children, I never believed my husband truly loved me. How could he love me? I still did stupid things. Oh how I loved my children, but I just knew in my heart that as they grew up, they would realize I was stupid and they wouldn't love me anymore.

Embarrassed and ashamed of my stupidity, I became quiet and withdrawn. I was afraid that if I talked to people they would quickly figure out my stupidity. I lived afraid of being found out. Silent and hurt, I learned to hide. No one around me knew what I was thinking or feeling. This is how the enemy works. He uses shame and fear to keep us quiet and alone.

So when I felt, saw, and breathed God's love into me, it literally changed my life. I was amazed that someone loved me. I absolutely fell in love with Him. At that moment I gained a father, brother, teacher, companion, and friend—not someone I read about, but someone I knew. He loved me with an incomprehensible love that I actually experienced. I was convinced that:

> ...neither death, nor life, nor angels, nor principalities, nor things present, nor things to come, nor powers, nor height, nor depth, nor any other created thing, will be able to separate [me] from the love of God, which is in Christ Jesus [my] Lord (Romans 8:38-39).

I can't say that overcoming rejection was instant for me at this point. However, this was the beginning of my healing process. I'm also not saying that it can't be instantaneous—it can—but for me it has been a process. It's very important to have our minds renewed (see Rom. 12:2) so that we believe the truth and not a lie. David wrote, "When my father and my mother forsake me, then the Lord will take me up" (Ps. 27:10 KJV).

Also, as I began to understand that my parents were raised in dysfunctional homes and were rejected themselves, it became much easier for me to forgive them. And forgiveness is the key. I, who has been forgiven so much, was able to forgive my parents for their seeming rejection of me. Now I know I have a Father in Heaven that absolutely loves me and will never reject me.

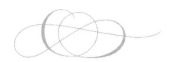

CHAPTER 4

LOVE ABOVE ALL

Once I discovered the purity of this always-and-forever love, I had to give it away to others. Now when I minister by leading groups into their own encounters with God, I'm surprised at the number of people who don't understand how much their God, their Father, loves them. Somehow religion has us believing what the enemy says instead of God's Word. If we focus on some of the harsher Old Testament Scriptures, we can view God as vengeful and punishing. If we ignore the Scriptures that demonstrate and declare God's love for us, forgetting we live under the New Covenant of grace, we turn God into a disciplinarian instead of the lover of our very beings. Paul the apostle states that God values love above all.

If I speak with the tongues of men and of angels, but do not have love, I have become a noisy gong or a clanging cymbal. If I have the gift of prophecy, and know all mysteries and all knowledge; and if I have all faith, so as to remove mountains, but do not have love, I am nothing. And if I give all my possessions to feed the poor, and if I surrender my body to be burned, but do not have love, it profits me nothing. Love is patient, love is kind and is not jealous; love does not brag and is not arrogant, does not act unbecomingly; it does not seek its own, is not provoked, does not take into account a wrong suffered, does not rejoice in unrighteousness, but rejoices with the truth; bears all things, believes all things, hopes all things, endures all things. Love never fails.... But now faith, hope, love, abide these three; but the greatest of these is love (1 Corinthians 13:1-8,13).

Love

The greatest of these is love, but somehow we question His love. Does He really love me? I'm not even close to perfect, and it's easy to feel inadequate and guilty about not being good enough. But God loves me and I can say along with Paul:

Not that I have already obtained it or have already become perfect, but I press on so that I may lay hold of that for which also I was laid hold of by Christ Jesus. Brethren, I do not regard myself as having laid hold of it yet; but one thing I do: forgetting what lies behind and reaching forward to what lies ahead, I press on toward the goal for the prize of the upward call of God in Christ Jesus (Philippians 3:12-14).

It is so wonderful that God's Word says He loves me, *"See how great a love the Father has bestowed on us, that we would be called children of God; and such we are..."* (1 John 3:1). But I know God loves me, not just because His Word says so, but because I've heard Him say He loves me.

I love words. Bernie Ooley, a wonderful Bible teacher at Bethel School of Supernatural Ministry (BSSM), said that words are like packages and you have to unwrap them. Have you ever thought about what *patience* really means? It's "the quality of enduring, constant in pursuit, persevering, calmly diligent."[1] God pursues us because He loves us so. Or consider *kindness:* "showing tenderness or goodness, disposed to do good and confer happiness, averse to hurting or paining." That is our God—patient and kind.

If you want to see into this Heaven realm, you have to believe in His patience and kindness. Otherwise you will be fearful of Him. If you don't take into account all that Jesus has done for you, fear will punish you. It is important that you don't take His kindness, tolerance, and patience lightly. For it is the kindness of God that leads us to repentance (see Rom. 2:4).

Kindness

When I feel the need to repent, I remember it is God's kindness and goodness leading me to change, not His judgment or harshness. God is so kind. He does not want to hurt me and He has a non-threatening way of showing me when I'm wrong. I remember one day He brought me to a place in the spirit realm that had a huge stairway reaching up very high. I could barely see the top. After straining to see what was at the top of the staircase, I realized I was seeing a door. I love to see new places and so I started climbing...and climbing...and climbing. It seemed like it took forever. It felt like I wasn't making any progress. Eventually I reached the top of the staircase. I was about to open the door and see what delights were on the other side when the Father said, "Oh, I'm sorry, but you can't go in there."

Can't go in there? I thought. *Here I've been climbing these stairs for such a long time. I've finally arrived at the top only to be told I can't go in there?* "But why?" I asked.

The Lord said, "Because you are angry with someone." As soon as He said it I knew exactly what He meant. Earlier that day something had happened and I had become angry with someone. I realized that right at that moment I still carried anger.

The truth struck me that my sin can keep me from walking into new places that the Lord wants to show me. The Lord didn't get angry with me or chide me. He quietly and gently told me about something that was keeping me from walking into another adventure with Him.

It is so much easier to repent when you don't feel that God is mad at you. He never has to be harsh because He loves us and wants the best for us. That's a love relationship. The primary reason I repent, or change the way I think, is because my Father has told me to do so, not because I know that is what the Bible states I must do. I've come to the realization that Jesus paid a huge price for me, and my Holy Spirit only wants to lead me into righteous paths and comfort me along the way.

Walk on with me. There is so much more to discover in this Kingdom of pure love. But first, let's hurdle past some obstacles so that you can begin to see what lies inside this Kingdom of love.

Endnote

1. "patience." *Microsoft Word Dictionary*. 2008, version 12.2.4.

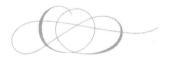

CHAPTER 5

You Can See

I believe that you can see into the heavenly realms by using your spiritual eyes. Ephesians 1:18 says:

I pray that the eyes of your heart may be enlightened, so that you will know what is the hope of His calling, what are the riches of the glory of His inheritance in the saints.

I like that part about the hope of His calling and the riches and inheritance, but what really catches my attention is "eyes of your heart." These aren't the "eyes of our head," which are natural abilities to comprehend the natural world (though sometimes we see supernatural things—like angels—with our natural eyes). Rather these are eyes that have spiritual perception. They perceive natural and supernatural things.

What do you think Paul is saying? I think he's saying that he wants the eyes of our spirit to be opened. Does your spirit really have eyes? In his book *Discovering the Seer in You*, James Goll states:

> Every born-again believer has two sets of eyes. We have our physical eyes, with which we view the physical world around us. In addition, the apostle Paul talks about a second set of eyes—the eyes of our heart that can be enlightened to perceive spiritual truth.[1]

Jesus repeatedly said, *"He who has ears to hear, let him hear"* (see Matt. 11:15; Mark 4:9,23; 7:16; Luke 8:8; 14:35). So, our ears are to hear. I know some people are deaf, but the vast majority of us can hear. So what did He mean by this? Could He be talking about our spiritual (spirit) ears?

First Corinthians 14:2 reminds us, *"...one who speaks in a tongue does not speak to men but to God; for no one understands, but in his **spirit** he speaks mysteries."* First Corinthians 14:14 explains that when we speak in tongues our spirit is speaking. We know that we are spirit, because Romans 8:16 states, *"The Spirit Himself testifies with our spirit that we are children of God."* And First Corinthians 2:11 states, *"For who among men knows the thoughts of a man except the spirit of the man which is in him?"*

In addition to our spirit, we know we each have a body. And we know we each have a soul, which is our intellect, will, and emotions. James 2:26 states, *"For just as the body without the spirit is dead, so also faith without works is dead."*

The Supernatural Realm

Do you understand what can happen with your spirit in the spirit realm? You can actually internally see, hear, and speak with your spiritual eyes, ears, and voice. As I began to grasp this concept, it began to make more sense to me. I have often found this concept to be an obstacle to those who want to see into the spiritual realm but have difficulty doing so. You first have to realize that it's not unlike seeing with our imaginations. Bob Jones, the prophet, uses the term "sanctified imagination." Pastor Bill Johnson says, "A sanctified imagination positions you for dreams and visions."

To imagine, you form an image of something in your mind. You actually use your mind to see something that is unreal. What I'm talking about here isn't something that you make up in your mind; it's something you observe that didn't come from your mind. It's something you experience. In Discovering the Seer in You, James Goll states, "I am convinced that any believer can develop the seer capacity."[2]

Now, I can hear people say "That's just vain imagination and you'll go into error if you imagine stuff." I agree that there is a danger of error if we imagine things. But there is also a danger of missing out on incredibly powerful and godly experiences because of the fear of being deceived. There is also a danger in calling something unclean God has called clean.

I think my spirit has truly been made alive and my mind has been washed with the Word. Without claiming any sort of personal sinlessness or perfection concerning seeing in God's realm, I do think my sin nature has been crucified with

Christ. It is not normal for me to sin (see Rom. 6). Sure, I can still do it (much to my chagrin) but it is no longer natural for me. So I have a great deal of trust in what Jesus did on the cross for us. With a renewed mind and heart and my spirit made alive and the Holy Spirit indwelling me forever, I have confidence that He can lead me.

Furthermore, Scriptures activate our imaginations all the time. The prophets and psalmists created plenty of images. For example, I can only "see" Zechariah's flying scroll by letting pictures move before my mind's eye (see Zech. 5). The Lord's prophets called Israel to imagine the judgment coming on them if they didn't return to the covenant and to imagine the blessings if they did. God was hoping this information and the mental pictures it created would move them to repentance. Imagination is just another access point for the Lord to reach us, as are language and music.

I am aware of some of the discussions among prophets about who has the right to initiate these sorts of heavenly experiences—God or us. This concern usually arises when I help lead people as they make themselves available for God to communicate with them in this way. It seems plain that God has the right to do so. And we all suppose that we are quite comfortable with this until someone begins to say he had a vision—then we get nervous! Can we initiate these sorts of experiences? I think we can at least ask and make ourselves available. As you will see from the stories that follow of my heavenly visions, my own experience is that sometimes they catch me by surprise and other times I am praying and waiting and hoping I get caught "by surprise."

Are these heavenly visions of the same type as people in the Bible experienced? Do they compare with Paul's experience of being caught up in the Third Heaven or with Ezekiel's visions? Well, they compare, but I don't claim that the things I am seeing and saying are on any level of inspired authoritative Scripture. Truthfully, I have seen some things I don't understand and won't share until I do. I do not make a new doctrine or theology out of them. I just saw them. In the pages ahead I will share with you times when I thought I had ruined everything by seeing something I shouldn't, but then the Holy Spirit communicated with me that it was OK.

In Scripture there seems to be different sorts of supernatural experiences and visions. I, and I would expect others, have had a variety of heavenly experiences. During some of them it feels like I could "come out of it" whenever I want; other times I am lost in the experience. Always though, it feels like I am "going" somewhere, if that makes sense. And I am being led, rather than leading, though I am free to ask questions and make requests, so it could be said that I am initiating some of the "action."

In short, God and I partner in these times. In a few pages I will share some of my "journeys." They may read as simple stories but they have all had a deeply profound impact on me, and they serve as examples of the sorts of experiences that may await you.

What About Deception?

At first I was worried about being deceived. So one day I talked to Bill Johnson about my concern. He responded by saying, "Then your God is too small and your devil too big." I realized that I loved the Father, Jesus, and the Holy Spirit, and that the Holy Spirit was my Guide and my Teacher. I trust Him to lead me in righteous paths, and I stay accountable to those who are in my life. I know the Word. So I'm no longer afraid of being deceived. Fear comes from the enemy, and he doesn't want us to experience God. And the truth is that Jesus knows my heart and is more than able to keep me in His ways. Jude 1:24 states:

> *Now to Him who is able to keep you from stumbling, and to make you stand in the presence of His glory blameless with great joy.*

Is it possible that someone will be deceived or "go off the deep end"? Sure, but what's not to say they would do so anyway? People can twist just about anything and become deceived. We can't be so afraid of going into error that we "throw the baby out with the bathwater." We have to learn to eat the meat and spit out the bones. Bill Johnson says, "Overreacting to error often leads to more error." Ultimately, we are responsible for ourselves. It's important that we don't become afraid of someone who thinks differently from us and stumble over something that is meant for our good.

Endnotes

1. James Goll, *Discovering the Seer in You*, (*Destiny Image Publishers, Inc., 2007*), 13.

2. Ibid.

CHAPTER 6

HURDLING OBSTACLES TO SEEING

Childlike Faith

So how do you learn to see with the eyes of your spirit? You approach Him with childlike faith and trust and know that He will embrace you and draw you in. Mark 10:15 states, *"Truly I say to you, whoever does not receive the kingdom of God like a child will not enter it at all."* Now we might think that this refers to going to Heaven after we die, but Jesus said "the Kingdom is at hand" (see Matt. 3:2; 4:17; 10:7; Mark 1:15). The Kingdom is here and it's for now. The truth is that we need a childlike attitude now. If you think about it, God created this planet, setting up the order He desired. Then the man He created rebelled and God had to send Jesus to rescue us from our folly. In all of this He is called Father and we are called children.

First, we trust that our Father only wants the best for us, just as we only want the best for our children. Therefore we know that whatever He asks us to do is for our own good. Think about it. Do you ever ask your children to do something that is not in their best interest? Would you ask your child to do something that could cause her physical or emotional harm? Of course not. How much more our Father in Heaven loves us! I love to watch the faces of my children when they open the good gifts I give them. I get as much pleasure from their joy as they get from receiving the gifts. Our Father desires to give us good things. He is more than ready to give us the tools we need to do the work He's asked us to do. Are you getting the picture?

Although I can't give you any statistics, I have found that people who are unable to be childlike in their attitude toward God have the most difficulty experiencing Him in any way. I'm not saying we shouldn't be mature. In actuality, the mature believer will trust the Father and will guard his heart, keeping it childlike.

Believe That You Are Forgiven and Forgive

The biggest obstacle to encountering God is believing in His complete forgiveness. We say we believe in the doctrine of forgiveness, but we have not captured the truth of forgiveness in our hearts. And although we try to "fake it," our unbelief is reflected in our attitudes and behaviors. Because we don't believe in our complete forgiveness, we then have difficulty believing we are "good" enough to get close to Jesus. Not believing we're "good" enough is the companion obstacle to not feeling forgiven.

I've prayed with numerous people who can see Jesus "far off" in the distance, but when I ask them to draw closer to Jesus they are unable to do so. At this point I stop and ask them if they have any unforgiveness in their heart for others or themselves. Isn't it sad that we think we've committed too many wrongs to draw near to Jesus? I once prayed with a girl who saw herself in a scene with Jesus looking out at the beauty of Heaven. When I asked her where Jesus was, she said He was standing behind her. I asked her to turn around, but she couldn't seem to do so. She finally began to cry, telling me that she was afraid if she turned around, Jesus wouldn't be there. As I prayed with her she revealed that she had been abandoned by her dad when he left the family and she put that same fear of abandonment on Jesus. As much as she loved Jesus, she felt that He wouldn't be there for her.

A Needed Lesson

I recall a time when I did something that caused some people to be hurt by my actions. When I realized what I had done, I went to them and asked forgiveness. They forgave me with no hesitation. That night as I was sitting talking to the Father about this situation, He said something that I thought sounded harsh. I put my head down as a child would when being scolded. The Father leaned over to me with His face close to mine and said so very kindly, "Don't ever attribute that tone of voice to Me; I only speak to you with loving-kindness."

I was dumbfounded. I said to Him, "Do you mean to tell me that I can change the way I hear You depending on how I feel about myself, or how I think You should feel about me?" This really opened up understanding to me. The next day, as I was talking to Bill Johnson about this, he reminded me of a Scripture in John 12:28-29:

> *"Father, glorify Your name." Then a voice came out of heaven: "I have both glorified it, and will glorify it again."* **So the crowd of people who stood by and heard it were saying that it had thundered; others were saying, "An angel has spoken to Him."**

So although everyone heard something, some people were "impaired" in their hearing. What they heard was dependent upon whom they believed Jesus to be.

When Jesus died on the cross, He made a full and complete payment for each and every sin. There is nothing we can add to what He's already done! So His voice should only be heard as a voice that is filled with loving-kindness.

Why don't you stop right here and think of any sin that may be holding you back, any sin that makes you feel ashamed. Maybe you've asked forgiveness 100 times before. Deal with it now. That sin was buried in the grave along with Jesus; however, when Jesus was resurrected, your sin was not! Hallelujah! Jesus never goes back to the grave to see what's in it and neither should we. God said that *He remembers it no more!* (see Heb. 8:12; 10:17).

As a side note to forgiveness, after He talked to me about the way He speaks to me, I was thinking that I should at least hang my head around the people I had hurt. After all, I wanted them to know I was really sorry. Instantly the Lord said, "If you do that, you are putting the importance of their forgiveness over the importance of Mine. I forgave you, even if they didn't. You are forgiven and you should act like it." Let me tell you, it was not easy going to church the next morning behaving as if I had done nothing wrong. I was afraid they would think I wasn't really sorry. I was afraid...Fear of man is not a good thing to carry around.

Another obstacle to experiencing God's presence is being offended at God. Now people can say they aren't offended at God, not recognizing their feelings of hurt as an offense toward God. We know He's perfect in all of His ways, and we try to talk our way out of it, but we hurt. In our pain we just don't trust Him to do something we ask. Oh we still ask, but there is disbelief in our asking.

We think, *Why would God show me anything heavenly when He didn't even answer my other prayer, which was far more important?* We need to answer that in our hearts. Everyone has prayers that have remained unfulfilled, but are we going to respond like David did? *"Trust in the Lord with all your heart and do not lean on your own understanding"* (Prov. 3:5). Or are we going to go into offense?

Let Go of Shame

We need to let go of our shame. As I said earlier, the enemy used shame to keep me quiet. Because of my embarrassment and shame about feeling stupid, I became quiet and withdrawn. I didn't want to talk to people because ultimately I was afraid they would reject me. Letting go of shame is a companion to forgiveness. Part of forgiving ourselves is letting go of shame. Jesus does not shame us and we want to represent Him accurately. So when we forgive ourselves and let go of shame, we show the world the greatness of His love. We truly are forgiven and we need to act like it!

CHAPTER 7

HE WILL NEVER REJECT YOU

Rejection is another obstacle that keeps us from receiving His love and seeing Him with the eyes of our spirit. One day God gave me a vision that not only healed my sense of rejection but brought me into a greater understanding of His amazing love. In this vision, I saw my mother on the birthing table giving birth to me. She was covered with a sheet and across the sheet was written the word *Rejection*. This made sense to me because my mother had lived a very hard life as one of nine children during the Depression. She had to quit school to work and help support her family. Her dad was an angry man who beat her mother and all of the children.

In the vision I then watched as I was born. As the doctor held me I saw the word *Rejection* written on me. At the time of this vision, I realized that this was a generational curse.

Part of the weight of rejection that I carried was a result of my mother passing it on to me. But I didn't know what to do with this information, and it wasn't until later that I understood how to be delivered from this curse.

I flew back to Toronto Airport Christian Fellowship to attend a conference. As I was lying down in my hotel room before the first meeting of the conference, this same vision came to me again. I saw my mother on the birthing table and again I could see myself being born. On both of us was that word, *Rejection.* But something was different this time. In the previous vision I only had seen the doctor's arms holding me. This time the "camera" panned up and I saw that it was Doctor Jesus holding me. He smiled at the baby as He pulled the word *Rejection* off of me, and then His gaze came up. He looked me square in the eyes and He smiled at me. What a Savior. What a wonderful, wonderful Healer. I thought that was the end of it, but He had even a more complete healing planned for me that trip.

Just a Whisper

On the next to the last night of that conference, I was sitting across from my friend Claudia Perry on the shuttle bus that was taking our group back to the hotel. Claudia called my name, and as I leaned over to look at her, she mouthed the words, "I love you." It was nothing dramatic, but I felt like I had been hit right in my heart. I closed my eyes, wondering what was happening as His presence grew stronger. Everyone got up and off the shuttle, but I had a hard time standing. I was doubled over as I walked into the hotel. When I got to the elevators and leaned against the wall, I realized that all of my motor skills were shutting down. I heard some of the group calling my name, but I couldn't answer. Claudia's husband, Bob, a tall man, came up behind me and guided me into the elevator. As he let go of me I fell to the floor. My pastors, Bill and Beni Johnson, and four other couples were present, and you would think I would have been embarrassed. However, all I could do was wonder what was God doing with me. They ended up carrying me to my room and laying me on my bed, and then left me there as they went to dinner.

After they left, God came. The room disappeared, and there I was with both the Father and Jesus. I saw a huge paper and it started to burn in the middle. As I watched it burn, I realized that it represented the lie that I believed, the lie of being unlovable. Oh, I believed that God loved me. I had experienced God's love. But could people love me? No, I was still stupid. So even though I knew God loved me, I didn't believe people could love me as well. However, the lie that I had believed was burning away. Perhaps you've also experienced what it's like for God to expose a lie you've believed to be true. It's hard to believe that you carried such deep-seated thoughts of feeling unlovable and rejected for so long and it wasn't even true!

Then the Father reached in and took my heart in His hands. He and Jesus were looking at my heart, and I noticed part of it was black. I knew that the black part of my heart was the area that had been so hurt and damaged. The Father took His hand, cut off the damaged part, and threw it away. Then He reached into His own heart and took some of His heart, joined it to mine, and put it back in my body. Now I have part of His heart beating in mine.

I can tell you, I didn't want to come back from that place of being with Him. To be in His presence, to be with Him, is the ultimate joy. It is also the place of ultimate freedom from all that holds us back.

Over and over I have told people that He wants to be with them more than they want to be with Him. **He will never reject you!** He is waiting to meet you in a new way, a more personal way. It was never God's intention to get a mail-order bride for His Son. When we receive Him as our Savior, He comes and dwells in us. This is the point at which the Bride and her Groom start their relationship and their union is consummated. From that point forward we go on with Him, developing a closer and deeper relationship with our Groom, discovering the mysteries of Him, and, dare I say, Him finding out about us.

What a great journey this is. It's so exciting that every day we can be with Him.

CHAPTER 8

SITTING ON THE FATHER'S LAP

I want to repeat what I said just a bit earlier: God always has more for us. God has more for you! Above all, He wants to give you His *friendship.* This is the true purpose for Christ's sacrifice on the cross. He created a way for us to be reunited with our Father, and it is as we learn to walk in relationship with Him that the full effect of salvation—the healing of our souls, spirits, and bodies—begins to manifest in our lives. We don't have to wait to finish our life on this earth before we begin to experience intimacy with God and the restoration that comes with it.

But God doesn't want to just heal us. The *more* that God had for me was not simply undoing the brokenness in my life.

He wanted to replace it with the thing He had intended for me from the beginning—a relationship with Him in which He shares who He is with me so that I can know Him, become like Him, and partner with Him in history.

Clearly, visions played an enormous role in my healing journey. But the rest of the story is that God brought me into these visionary experiences primarily as His way of relating with me, as you will see. This dimension of my relationship with God opened up to me in February of 1997 before my first trip to Toronto. At that time I was reading a book about prayer called *Beyond the Veil* by Alice Smith, which was about getting closer to God. The title refers to the picture in Scripture of the Tabernacle of Moses and the Temple, where the presence of God was kept behind a veil in the Holy of Holies. This veil was torn at Christ's death, signifying that we need no longer be kept from the presence of God but are invited to have a relationship with Him for ourselves. Well, the Lord began to invite me beyond the veil.

One night I went to bed and as I began to pray, I could see a door open partway. At that point in my life I didn't know it was possible for me to know His presence like that. I had never felt anything like it before. It was so sweet and so holy.

As I experienced His presence, I stopped praying because all I wanted to do was to worship Him. With this amazing awareness of Him came the absolute knowledge of how great and awesome He is. This continued to happen every night—me starting to pray, only to have the door open a bit and finding I could not stop myself from worshiping God. I was compelled to worship because the atmosphere was so magnificent. Part of the word *worship* means "to kiss."

Open Door

Then in May of 1997, right after that first trip to Toronto, I started to pray one night when the partially opened door suddenly swung wide open. I found myself in a place with two figures standing in front of me. When the door first opened, I could only see "through a glass darkly" and I could not distinguish details or features (see 1 Cor. 13:12 KJV). There was no real color, just a foggy grayness. I did know that the two images I saw were the Father and Jesus. In that first experience beyond the door, I simply stood before them and talked with them.

Every time I prayed I would find myself in this same place. One day I felt a little discouraged and I asked the Father if He would give me a hug—not really thinking that anything would happen or be different than the usual foggy state of the vision. But at that point things became clearer, the grayness dissipated, and my "eyes" were able to see things more clearly. I saw then that God was on a throne, and the left side of the throne had steps leading up to the Father.

Into His Lap

When I saw this, I ran and climbed up the steps and sat on His lap. In the vision I was the size of a four-year-old in comparison to His adult size. In fact, for the first couple of years in all of my visions I appeared as a little girl, even though my mind was in my present adult state. I tried to wrap my arms around His middle but my arms only came halfway to His sides, like trying to buckle a seat belt with only half of the belt. Then He wrapped His arms around me. I actually felt His arms—not just the sensation of being touched, but the substance and weight of His arms around me. Never before had I felt such peace and love. It was tangible.

During subsequent visions with Him, I found myself sitting in His lap—me loving Him and Him loving me. How content I was to be there, knowing that nothing mattered but this togetherness. Of course I thought that I was just imagining all of it. After all, who sits on God's lap and talks to Him? But I didn't care at all. I physically felt His love and the deep pleasure He took in me being there with Him. Whenever I was upset or out of sorts about something, all it took to get a proper perspective was to be with Him. He was God. He had the answers and I trusted Him.

I couldn't find anything in the Word that said what I was experiencing was wrong. So the visions grew more and more real to me. I wondered if I was just imagining these times, but the experiences occurred in such a fashion that I had no forethought as to what was going to happen next. During these experiences I checked my heart constantly. I had more checks on myself than there are in the mail, and yet I seemed to know that it could not be anything but right. It was the right place to be for the rest of my life.

CHAPTER 9

RUN INTO THE LIGHT

Although I knew I was in the right place, at some point I started to get restless. I knew there was more and this throne room place was just a beginning. There was so much more knowledge of Him for me to have. I wanted to know His heart. Moses met God face to face and he knew His ways, not just His deeds (see Ps. 103:7). So one day I stood up on God's lap and put my arms around His neck with my face next to His and my mouth next to His ear. I whispered, "My Father, I want to go deeper in You." Then I turned my head and kissed His cheek.

This asking to go deeper continued for about a month. It got to the point where I was begging Him to take me deeper, just like a child tugging at her Daddy's arm, "Can I, can I, can I, huh?" At one point I stood before the throne, grabbed

Jesus' hand, pulled Him over, and said, "Father, I want to go deeper with You. I am praying this prayer and Jesus, who is interceding for me, is agreeing with my words." I continued beseeching God, "I know this is OK because it is Your will that we pursue You. So Father, Jesus and I are in agreement for this to be done."

My Father replied with a simple, "OK." *OK*—just like it was nothing and that this was the first time I had made that particular request.

God showed me the kingdom of darkness, and between the kingdom of darkness and the Kingdom of Light was a huge chasm. There was a bridge over the chasm and I knew what this meant. The bridge was Jesus. A lot of people were standing on the bridge, and they represented all those who had accepted Jesus as their Savior but had never moved from that place. They never really entered into the Kingdom of Light.

God showed me that I was not on the bridge. I was in the Kingdom of Light, but I was standing right beside the bridge, next to the chasm. Because I was so close to the kingdom of darkness, the enemy could shoot spit wads at me. While the wads didn't really hurt me when they splattered on my skin, they were gross and I was constantly picking off the slimy, sloppy things (shudder). Once in a while a rock was thrown at me, but the distance was great and there wasn't enough momentum for the rocks to really hurt me. Even so, it was annoying and sometimes the rocks had sharp points that nicked me. This didn't cause me much pain, but it was a nuisance.

Run!

The Lord told me to run into the Kingdom of Light. I started to run as fast as I could. The terrain was hilly, more like mounds, and it was so bright that I wished I had my sunglasses with me. The ground was the color of maize and the sky was a startling celestial blue. I ran and ran, but I couldn't see anything. Finally I stopped and looked around, and as far as I could see was maize-colored ground and bright blue sky. The emptiness of the land and the absence of sound felt strange to me. There was a surreal sense about it, like walking into the foreground of a Salvador Dali landscape. Then I heard Him say again, "Run, run, run into the Kingdom of Light." So off I went again, running farther toward the horizon of yellow and blue.

I ran until I came upon my Father's throne, and there I found my Father, Jesus, and the Holy Spirit all dancing. The Holy Spirit was twirling around like a miniature tornado, spinning joy. The Father and Jesus were dancing a primitive-type dance that was full of passion and rejoicing. What a picture!

The Father's dance was rather undignified—certainly not a waltz by any means. I wondered, *How can I really be seeing the Maker of the Universe being so exuberant?* To tell the truth, I felt a little embarrassed. After His dance, my Father sat down on His throne and called me up to sit on His lap. He noticed my uneasiness and asked me what was wrong. Dispassionately I said, "Oh nothing." *Oh nothing?* Talk about a "Sarah moment"—my response was about as lame as Sarah denying to God that she laughed when He said she would bear a son at age 90 (see Gen. 18:12). He told me that I was to tell

Him what was wrong and I said I thought His dance was perhaps a bit undignified—after all, He was God. Oh how He laughed and threw His arms out, declaring enthusiastically, "I love to dance. I created the dance."

As soon as He said that, I completely understood in every part of me that it was all OK because He created the dance and He can dance any which way He chooses. *"But our God is in the heavens; He does whatever He pleases"* (Ps. 115:3). I remembered how David danced before the Ark of the Covenant in total abandon because he was so happy. Was this what God was doing? Was the Father showing His joy? I was so happy to be there and He was so happy that I was there too. Oh how we danced in our joy.

After this experience, the maize place became the place where I met my Father. But I still knew there was more. I knew it more deeply than ever before. So, very shortly after I came into the maize place, I climbed back on my Father's lap, stood and whispered in His ear, "I want to go deeper in You." He said, "OK." Instantly He took one hand, Jesus took the other, and with the Holy Spirit whirling and twirling and dancing, we all ran deeper into the Kingdom of Light.

CHAPTER 10

THE BEAUTIFUL GARDEN

After running for some distance we came to a garden that was incredibly beautiful. The colors were intense and indescribable, like nothing on this earth. There were plants and trees in the garden that I had never seen before. I knew you wouldn't find them in any botanical books here on earth. A stream ran through this garden and behind the plants and trees was a rocky wall, which I didn't pay much attention to at the time. Eventually, it became a very significant wall—for no image is wasted in the Kingdom. Everything you see, even if you feel like you are only imagining it, has significance. That is why it is important for you to know that you can go back to a scene during prayer, revisit it, and ask God to show you more about what you are seeing. I always take time to explore the garden and God always delights in revealing more of the hidden things in His Kingdom and the things within my heart.

The Holy Spirit came and sat with us in this beautiful place. Before, He had been energy personified, going here and there, dancing and twirling. Now He sat with us in the garden. His joy in what was going on was very evident in His demeanor.

From that point on, whenever I started to pray, I found myself in the garden. Again I wondered if I was just making this all up. So I decided to go back to the gray throne room and the maize Kingdom of Light. I discovered that although I could get to those places, I couldn't find God there. After that experiment, I went back to the garden and talked to the Father about all that I was seeing and experiencing. It is a place where I go often to meet with Jesus.

God's First Language

When God talks to me we rarely use words. Our Senior Associate Pastor at Bethel Church, Kris Vallotton, told the congregation in one of his messages that God's first language isn't English or French or German or any other earthly language. When he said that, I thought, *Well, of course!* But Kris didn't say what God's language was, and it so intrigued me that I started pondering it. I've come to the conclusion that God's language is simply communication. He will use whatever He wants to use so that you will understand what He is saying. Whenever God and I have talks, it is Spirit-to-spirit. No English words are exchanged, but I know everything He is saying to me. It's not that I can always hear what He is saying. Sometimes I allow too much of my circumstances to get in the way. And it's not that He is always answering everything I ask. Sometimes He doesn't answer right away. But He is always communicating to me how much He loves me and that He's there for me. All I have to do is listen with my spiritual ears.

I can remember when I first learned that He is always talking (after all, He is called the Word). As I talked with God in the garden, He communicated that I was not to go backward. I was to have more adventures and learn many new things by going forward. I wouldn't go on until I learned what I needed to learn, and if He led me back, it would be to continue whatever I needed to learn in that place. So I stayed in the colorful garden.

The Stream

One day while in the garden, I went over to the stream and dipped my hand in the water. I knew it was liquid because I could feel the silky wetness on my fingers, but it looked solid and unyielding as though it was made of glass. I was immediately reminded of Revelation 22:1:

> *Then he showed me a river of the water of life, clear*
> *as crystal, coming from the throne of God and of the*
> *Lamb.*

This stream wasn't just clear as crystal; it actually looked like liquid glass.

I went over to the stream, jumped in, and submerged myself. As the water surrounded me I could feel its weight and vitality. After I jumped in the water it felt much larger than a stream. The water started flowing faster and faster and I felt like I was going to be swept away in the current. There was nothing for me to grab ahold of that would keep me from being carried away. The water rushed over me like the white water of a fast river. When I finally got out of the river, my clothing was white, white, white—bright white! It reminded me of another verse in Revelation 3:5:

He who overcomes will thus be clothed in white garments; and I will not erase his name from the book of life, and I will confess his name before My Father and before His angels.

One

Day after day while meeting in the garden, I would find myself sitting on my Father's lap. Sometimes when I sat with the Father, I would look over and see Jesus. Other times I would be with Jesus and look over to see the Father. I asked Jesus once if He was sad when I was with the Father and if the Father was sad when I was with Him. Now you might not think that was a mature question, but I was ever the little girl when I was with Him. He smiled when I asked Him this and said, "Turn around and look at the Father." I turned and there I saw myself sitting on His lap! How could I be with Jesus and at the very same time be sitting with my Father? In John 10:30, Jesus says, *"I and the Father are one."* That is one of the mysteries that Paul wrote about so often in Ephesians. I no longer felt as though I was favoring one over the other, because They are One.

CHAPTER 11

RELEASED FROM STRONGHOLDS

If you recall, I mentioned earlier that when I first entered the beautiful garden I saw a wall behind the plants and trees. Looking at the wall, I kept thinking that if I wanted to go deeper in God I was going to have to scale that wall. So I kept looking at the wall, pacing along the length, sizing it up, trying to figure out how I could climb it.

As I considered the wall, the Holy Spirit started to talk to me about strongholds in my life. A stronghold is a place where a particular belief or set of beliefs is strongly defended or upheld. I sure didn't want strongholds of wrong beliefs in my life if they were keeping me from being closer to God, but I wasn't really sure how to get rid of them. I didn't even know what particular strongholds were in my life. About the same time I was pondering the wall puzzle, I was reading a book by Francis Frangipane called *The Three Battlegrounds*. Guess what a certain section of it addressed? That's right—strongholds! This helped confirm that God was dealing with this particular area in my life.

Before I finally faced the wall, I looked back at the way I had come and I saw the stream I had jumped over to reach the wall. Not only had I jumped over it, I had turned around and jumped back over it again and splashed my way back to the other side of the stream, getting deliriously soaking wet. I wanted to get in that stream as much and as often as possible. Why jump over it when I could slosh it all over me and carry it with me longer? So there I stood, dripping wet, facing my "stronghold" wall. And the Holy Spirit was there with me.

He showed me "hooks" in the wall and told me that these hooks were my strongholds and that I would have to tear them down. He began to name them and as He did, I knew that He was right about each one. I climbed up on an outcropping of rock along the wall and started to kick at one, but it was a rock-hard "handhold hook" and did not budge. The Holy Spirit came over to me and gave me a sword that was sharp and shiny. I knew this sword was the Sword of the Spirit, which is the Word of God (see Eph. 6:17). Wielding the sword the Holy Spirit had given me, I initiated an all-out assault on those strongholds. Calling them the names He gave me, I used the Word of God to cut them off. For example, I declared, "God has not given me a spirit of fear..." (see 2 Tim. 1:7) because one of my strongholds was fear.

The hooks came off so much easier with the use of the sword. I attacked them as I confessed them, and as I confessed them, God forgave me and cleansed me from all unrighteousness. When I was done I went over and drank from the stream and started to wash myself. I began to laugh, and suddenly what I had done seemed hilarious. I rolled around on the side of the bank laughing, drinking, and splashing the water on me. God the Father, Jesus, and the Holy Spirit were laughing also. His glory was in the stream. His glory was wonderful.

Tree of Life

I noticed that one particular tree in the garden was bigger than all the other trees, and I knew that this tree played a significant role in the garden. I asked my Father about the tree and He said it was the Tree of Life. *Oh,* I thought, *the one in the Garden of Eden.* Looking up into the branches of the Tree of Life, I could see fruit on them. I climbed up into the tree and the Holy Spirit came with me. How fun! He sat on one branch and I sat on another. "Eat the fruit," He said. I didn't know exactly what it all meant, but I ate anyway. The fruit looked a lot like a marshmallow and it felt like a fig without the seeds. I could eat and eat and not get full. If this was indeed the Tree of Life, then it was also the tree of truth. How could you ever get full of truth? Never, I say, never! So I continued to eat.

At different times throughout this vision of the tree, I would get down out of the tree to meet with the Father, Jesus, and the Holy Spirit. Each time They told me to eat more of the fruit that grew there. In fact, I was told to eat until all of the fruit was gone. One time I climbed up the tree and the

Holy Spirit came with me to help me pick the fruit. I leaned over and said, "Thank You," and kissed His cheek. I giggled and He started laughing. It was the most wonderful sound and it made me so glad to be there and to know Him. After I had picked the fruit, I went over to where Jesus was sitting and sat down by Him to eat it. I leaned my back against Him and He had His arm around me. Sigh. I honestly cannot describe how wonderful it felt to be there. Wonderful—full of wonder! *Wonder* means "amazed admiration or awe, especially at something very beautiful or new."[1] Wonder certainly describes what I was feeling at that moment.

The next time I came to talk with the Father and Jesus, I asked about the tree and what it meant, especially the significance of me having to eat all of the fruit. They told me, "Just eat it." So I ate more, even though I didn't understand. When I had eaten all of the fruit and the tree was empty, the tree instantly grew more fruit.

Double Door

A few days later, while back in the garden gathering more fruit, I saw a double door. When I asked about the door, I was told that it was the door to God's city. When I heard this, I immediately felt that I didn't want to go to this place. The fact that I felt this was really strange to me because I had been so willing to go and do everything else. If I truly believed this was of God, I should want to go, shouldn't I? I felt so much trepidation. Before I could enter this door, I had to go to my Father.

As uneasiness about the door came over me, I began to wonder once again if I was making this all up in my imagination. I knew that each day I was growing to love my Father, Jesus, and the Holy Spirit more and more. I desired to spend more time with Them, worshiping Them and tasting Their awesome love. My desire was to be conformed to the image of Christ, to let Jesus' light shine in me, to do my Father's will, and to follow the Holy Spirit. So why did I have uneasiness and doubts about my visions?

Father called me over to Him and asked me what was wrong. So I told Him that I doubted that all of this was real. I sat there with my head in my hands, thinking. He asked me again what was wrong. I told Him that I had a great fear that He would do something bad to me, or that I would go into deception, be crushed by it, and somehow be humiliated. He told me that this thinking was a stronghold of *distrust* and that I had to go to the wall and chop it down like the rest of the strongholds the Holy Spirit had shown me.

I went over to the wall and picked up the Sword of the Spirit. Very weakly and half-heartedly, I started to hack at the hook of distrust. This hook was bigger than all the rest of the strongholds I had dealt with so far, and my feeble chopping attempts did nothing to it. Father called me and I went back to Him. He beckoned me to sit on His lap and He asked me why I felt this way. I told Him I just didn't think I could ever measure up. Somewhere along the line I knew I would goof up really badly and He would be mad and do something to punish me.

Then I felt His love flowing through me like a sweet, warm river. I felt Jesus' love and I thought of His incredible sacrifice for me. The Holy Spirit drew near and I felt His loving compassion for my weakness during this time. That fear which caused my distrust was such a lie! God's love is much greater than the lies. How dare I believe such a lie, that my Father, my Jesus, my Holy Spirit would ever even think of doing something bad to me? *Well*, I thought, *even if I am imagining all of this, so what? I love God more. How could that be wrong?*

By then I was angered by the lie and I went over to the wall and took up my sword. I dealt it blow after blow and finally annihilated it as though it was warm wax. Then I went over to Jesus and kissed Him and told Him how grateful I was for Him. How amazingly wonderful and patient He was with me.

After this very emotional time, They told me to eat of the fruit in the tree again. I was learning always to eat from the Tree of Life. I had to eat all of the fruit from the tree because it was the fruit of knowing the truth. Today when I believe a lie, I think to myself, *From what tree am I eating?* That usually settles it for me. Romans 12:2 talks about the importance of renewing our mind. We need a renewed mind to not only recognize truth but to actually *live* out of that truth.

Strongholds Defeated

Now, these last few visions occurred over a three-day period. On Friday I knocked the strongholds down, ate all the fruit on Saturday, and started fighting the strongholds again on Sunday. Then on Sunday night I found the biggest stronghold of all—distrust! I spent all of Sunday morning battling all the strongholds I had already knocked down. Can you believe that? If I had knocked down all of the strongholds, why had they returned? I just didn't understand the nature of spiritual warfare. So I asked the Father about this. He told me that these strongholds were no longer present, but that I always needed to be on my guard, making sure that I did not give place for them to return, as the enemy is always trying to regain lost territory. The enemy was just trying to make me believe that the strongholds were still there and that the Spirit hadn't really shown me anything. He wanted me to think that what I had seen wasn't real, that somehow I had made it up in my own mind. I battled them with the Word, my Sword. Jesus had set me free, and therefore I was free indeed.

For three more days I battled—Sunday through Tuesday. Tuesday night at a prayer service I found it difficult to worship. I lay on my face talking to God about the double doors, my battle, and what I was to do. At the end of the worship time, God, my Father, Jesus, my love, and the Holy Spirit, all came around me and said in unison, "I love you." When the entire congregation came together to pray corporately, I was seized by laughter. I realize that people have criticized the laughter, but it's only because they have never truly experienced it. I really don't know how long I laughed, but I was sore by the time it was over. Never before had I laughed so hard. And by the time I was done laughing, the battle was over. I don't know how that works. How can laughter be warfare? I don't know, but one thing I do know is that I was victorious! I was ready to go through the double doors to God's city. I wanted to go, and I was waiting for what was to come next.

This victory through laughter confirmed a change that had already been happening in my heart. I was beginning to understand through these visions and experiences that the Holy Spirit is fun. He is like a child, taking delight in helping us and healing us physically and emotionally. When He brooded over the earth to bring forth life (see Gen. 1:1), He was having fun. He delights in every victory we have and He is part of every victory we have! He is excited by what God is doing and is going to do. He is free to be Himself. He yearns to have us grow into Jesus' image, and He wants to help us to be like Christ. He delighted in Jesus' life here on earth and rejoices that Jesus' Bride will soon come home to Him. He is the most positive influence on us. The Holy Spirit cheers us on! He's a joy. He's a giggle—He's my giggle!

Endnote

1. "wonder." *Microsoft Word Dictionary.* 2008, version 12.2.4.

CHAPTER 12

THE CITY OF GOD

Jesus came and asked me if I was ready to go into the City of God now. Unhesitatingly, I said, "Yes." But when I approached the double doors, I was a bit tentative in opening them. I felt as though I were getting ready to dive off the high diving board. You know that feeling—you want to make the dive, but you're just a little frightened about whether you will resurface in one piece. I finally took a deep breath and pushed open the door.

The Wind of Holiness

Everything was bright, clear, and white. I felt God's holiness everywhere. It was tangible and it rushed over me like a sudden wind. I felt my clothes pressed against my little body from this wind of holiness. I caught my breath and immediately dropped my head. I didn't belong in there—it was too holy. Jesus kept beckoning me in, saying, "Come in, come in."

I kept saying back to Him, "No, I can't."

He said, "Yes, you can."

But I wouldn't go. He came over and took my arm and gently pulled me in. I kept my head down and I told Him that I didn't belong there.

It was as though Jesus didn't even hear my protests. He asked me if I wanted to go deeper with God. I just couldn't ask, but He told me to go to the Father and ask to go deeper. As my head was down, I looked at His robe and I was struck by its whiteness. He told me to look at what I was wearing and I realized that my robe looked just like His. I still felt so unworthy and knew that this wonderful vision must end soon because He was just too holy for me to approach.

Jesus again urged me to ask my Father about going deeper with Him. I just shook my head, no. He then turned me toward the throne (the one with the steps on the side) and gently nudged me over to the bottom of the steps. Father then called to me and told me to come and sit with Him on His lap. I did so very slowly and with trembling. I sat hunched over like a child, a child who had done something wrong. He asked me what was wrong. I told Him I wasn't good enough to be there, and I felt so embarrassed because I didn't measure up.

Victory Over Unbelief

Father called Jesus over and He stood in front of me. He then told Jesus to stretch out His hands toward me. As He did, I saw the nail prints in His hands. Father told me if I believed that I didn't belong there with Him, then what I was saying was that what His Son did on the cross was for nothing. All His pain and all His suffering was for nothing. Did I believe that Jesus had lived, suffered, and died for nothing? I was instantly horrified. Never! Never would I nullify what Jesus had done for me. I realized that through His death, Jesus brought me to the place of fellowship with God. Jesus made me good enough.

I jumped down from my Father's lap and ran outside the double door, back to the wall. Then I picked up my sword and hacked away at the stronghold of unbelief—my unbelief about what Jesus' life and death had done for me and given me. I ran back into the city and boldly went up onto my Father's lap. This time I wrapped my arms around Him. Then I jumped down and ran over to Jesus, who bent down to me. Wrapping my arms around Him, I kissed Him on the cheek and told Him I knew that He had completed the work the Father had sent Him to do. I was worthy because of what He had done, and how I loved Him for it.

A little later, while I was sitting with the Father, He asked if I was ready for more understanding. He said there were many things that I had to learn. I noticed that behind the throne were pedestals with objects on each of them. Each object represented a lesson that He wanted me to learn. I thought He was going to show me around, but He called for the Holy Spirit to come and take me to the first object. I felt like the Holy Spirit was so pleased and delighted to be leading me. It was His pleasure to be with me.

CHAPTER 13

OBJECT LESSON OF REMEMBERING

Each of the pedestals in this place appeared to be made of white marble with gold veining. When I laid my hand upon a pedestal it felt elegantly smooth, but it was not cold to the touch. Each pedestal in this strange gallery was approximately the same in height and width.

The Holy Spirit led me to the first pedestal and told me to pick up an oval object that was on it. This object was about 1 foot in diameter and weighed about 1 pound. As I held this object, He told me, "Remember how you got here, so you can bring others."

I remembered that I had begun on the bridge at the edge of the Kingdom of Light and I had run into the light. This decision to go deeper into the Kingdom made me realize that this was why the Father, Jesus, and the Holy Spirit were so happy, dancing around, when I arrived at the throne in the maize-colored place. I had made the *best* decision, choosing God and leaving behind the kingdom of darkness. I forsook all at that point. But as I remembered this, something was happening in my spirit because I understood more of what my choice meant. I chose God! And I chose Him not for His blessings but because of my love for Him. I knew that with this choice would not only come blessing but also hardship. But the knowledge that there would be hardship really didn't matter at all to me because my desire to know Him more was so much stronger and more focused.

These things that I was seeing were strange, and I had to believe that God was leading me on this newest "going-deeper" trek. Because of my belief that God was in this, I knew that if I kept on with these journeys, I would learn a lot—I already had. Fear, I knew, was not from God, yet I had so much fear of being deceived. But I believed that my God was able to keep me from deception when my heart was for Him. Jude 1:24 states:

> *Now to Him who is able to keep you from stumbling, and to make you stand in the presence of His glory blameless with great joy.*

Remembering

Then I remembered that my visits to the maize place had lasted for about two weeks before I had asked to go further. Next had come the colorful garden. As I remembered the garden, I surveyed it once more and the Holy Spirit asked me, "What do you see?"

I saw the stream, the stronghold wall, the Tree of Life, and the empty throne (God was in the city). I didn't see anything that struck me or quickened my spirit. I asked Him, "What? What am I not seeing?"

Again He asked, "What do you see?"

As I walked over to the wall and looked again, I noticed that I couldn't even see where the stronghold hooks had been. It was as though they had never been there. But I knew they had been, for I had knocked them down. I looked at the glassy stream, but it was just flowing smoothly. Suddenly I wondered where the water was coming from, so I followed the stream. It was coming from God's throne in the city. Was this what I was to see? I climbed once again up into the Tree of Life, but there was nothing out of place or different.

"What is it, Holy Spirit? What am I to see?"

"You are to see what happened here," was His reply.

The visions all passed through my memory like an instant replay. I remembered how, with the Holy Spirit's help, I had chopped down the strongholds of fear, distrust, and unbelief. There had been other strongholds I had chopped down as well. I recalled how I had lain in the river and been cleansed, delivered, and healed. I had been so encouraged by my Father, and the Holy Spirit had become so real to me. Everything I did in the garden had helped me to realize my total dependency on God. I would not have been able to identify, much less chop down, any of the strongholds by myself. I would not have learned truth without God's patience and love. I truly became dependent on the Father, Jesus, and the Holy Spirit. How sufficient I am in Them, for They are my comfort and refuge.

This journey of seeing and understanding more as I reviewed my experiences continued. I remembered how I had finally become ready to go into the city. This had been a hard step for me because of my overwhelming feelings of unworthiness. My heart had hurt because I had felt and believed that I was at the end of my wonderful journey. But what did I learn? I *knew* without a shadow of doubt, that my wonderful Jesus had paid the price for me. This price that my Jesus paid did it **all**. Not one thing was left that He had not purchased for me. I am under His wing, I am chosen, and I am His! I have become His righteousness, His worthiness, and His image before my Father. There is no room for shame because there is no shame. I can come to my Father boldly because I have become and I am becoming just like Jesus.

Eating the Lesson

After remembering *how* I had come to this place as the Holy Spirit had instructed me, I found myself with Him in the city again. I was still holding the object and the Holy Spirit told me to eat the object. As I began to eat it, I found it was delicious—sweet and crunchy. After about three bites it turned into a thick liquid, like honey. I was eating it as fast as I could because I didn't want any of it to spill on the ground. I even licked my fingers and face after it was all gone.

At this point I found that I was quite sticky. I asked the Holy Spirit if this stickiness would go away or if I should go wash it off. He told me to go wash off in the river that was flowing from God's throne. So I went over and stood by the river. As I looked up at my Father and Jesus, They began to laugh because of the sticky residue all over my face and hands. I thought I probably looked like a child who had been in the cookie jar and had chocolate all over her face. Well, They were delighted because I had *lesson* all over my face. I had earnestly eaten all of the *lesson*, even licking the bits off my hands and face, and this so pleased the Father and Jesus that They broke out in laughter and delight.

CHAPTER 14

MORE OBJECT LESSONS

A very short time later I was sitting with my Father and He asked me if I was ready for another "object lesson." I wondered perhaps if I was moving too fast. Always before when I had learned something, the lesson had been followed by an extended time of experiencing what I had learned. God told me that because I had eaten the first object—consumed it—it would be with me. I understood that time is short and He is doing something new in His children. He is doing instant things. However, it is important that we not misunderstand—we must realize that we have to take responsibility for what He is showing us and that some things may still take time.

Protection

With that, I was ready for the next lesson. The Holy Spirit took me to another pedestal, which held an object about the size of a golf ball. I picked it up and held it expectantly. I stood there, staring at nothing and seeing nothing happen. I asked the Holy Spirit what it was, and as soon as I had spoken the words, the object started to expand in my hand. It was a strange sensation, as though it were alive. The object grew and covered me like a transparent cocoon. When I again asked what this was, I was told that it was *protection.* I wondered how I should put it on. I was thinking I should put it on like armor. He then promptly told me, "It *is* on," and He instructed me to never take it off. This object was to remind me that every time I was hit by a fiery dart from the enemy, any accusation, any fear, or any lie, I was to go immediately, immediately, immediately to the throne room and talk with my God about it. I was never to take my protection off, never even to think that I could handle a dart on my own. I always need to be dependent on my Father, Jesus, and the Holy Spirit to tell me the truth.

Petals

The next pedestal held an object that was round and smooth, about the size of a bowling ball. It felt exceedingly good in my hands, almost like a long-forgotten favorite toy from my childhood. The Holy Spirit told me to hold it tight. So I held it as tight as I could and then Jesus came and pushed it inside of my chest. It just slipped inside as easily as swallowing warm melted chocolate. I looked down and I could see it there inside me. Amazingly, it started to bloom. It became a rose, unfolding its glory petal by petal, just like you see in a time-lapse film. After the rose had bloomed, Jesus reached inside of me and took a petal, laid it on the marble step, and crushed it under His foot. I was a bit surprised when He did this, but I felt that whatever He was doing was significant and He would let me know the reason soon enough. I reached down and gathered up all the little pieces of the crushed petal. As I stood up, I noticed that I was now wearing a long white coat with little pockets all over it. I put the crushed petal in one of the pockets.

After I placed the petal pieces in my pocket, Jesus reached in and took another petal, laid it on the step, and crushed it. Again I bent down, scooped the pieces up and put them in one of the many wonderful pockets of my coat. Jesus continued to do this until all of the petals were gone and all of my pockets were full. He told me that the petals represented His love. The Scripture in Isaiah 53:5 came to mind, *"But He was pierced through for our transgressions, He was crushed for our iniquities...."* Then I remembered that when you take a flower and crush the petals, the fragrance is released more fully. How often while walking along have I plucked a leaf from a bush and rubbed it between my fingers, releasing the aroma and smelling it on my fingers until I washed my hands. You see, God has always loved us—always! But when Jesus was crushed and died for our sins, His love was released even more.

Jesus then told me what would happen when I wore this coat in public. He said that as I walked along, someone would pass me, then stop, turn around, come back to me, and say, "Excuse me, but that is a wonderful fragrance you have on. Would you mind telling me the name of it and where I might purchase some for myself?" Jesus said that I could tell the person, "Oh, it is a wonderful fragrance. It's the fragrance of God's love. And I can tell you where you can get some, but you don't have to pay any money for it. You see, the price has already been paid."

I looked down at the place where Jesus had taken the petals from the rose inside of me. I thought that I might have an empty hole or maybe just a bare stem where the rose had been, but there at the heart of all of the petals of love was a pearl. The pearl was gorgeously smooth and milky in color. I knew that this pearl was the pearl of great price.

The coat of the fragrance of God's love didn't have buttons, ties, or a zipper. Jesus showed me that in my everyday busy life I might let the coat slip off. He said I must be careful always to keep my coat on so people could be exposed to the attractive fragrance of love. I took His instruction to heart, but I also wondered what would happen if I did let it slip off for some reason. Jesus is so absolutely wonderful to me. He then showed me that when my coat slipped off, the Holy Spirit would come along, pick it up, and follow me around, calling my name until I stopped and let Him help me put it on again. Isn't He wonderful?

The Marble Bench

During a Friday night worship service at Bethel, the Holy Spirit came to me and asked me to follow Him. He took me back to the place of the pedestals and there in the midst of all of them was a lovely marble bench. I sat down in the very middle of the bench with my hands resting on both sides. As I sat there, I waited and listened expectantly, for I thought He was going to speak to me and teach me something. I closed my eyes and waited.

Jesus came over to the bench and said, "Make room for Me." My eyes popped open. I instantly scooted over and He sat down with me. I bent my head in concentration; I didn't want to miss what He was going to say to me. But He was so quiet that I finally turned and looked up at Him and asked Him what the lesson was. Jesus said, "Make room for Me. When you clean your room, make room for Me. When you wash the dishes, make room for Me. When you drive your car, make room for Me. When you calculate the payroll (my job at the time), make room for Me." Jesus looked directly into my eyes and said, "Judy, make room for Me in everything you do."

The Golden Egg

Throughout these past few months I had been praying that I would come to know the heart of God. Somehow I knew that God would use the next object to answer my request because this was my heart's desire. Of course, I didn't know then what the object would be, but I have since realized that what I was feeling was true.

The next object I saw on the pedestal was the size of an egg. Oh what an egg! It was both crystal and golden—crystal gold—and it had so many facets. I simply held it for several days because nothing else was said to me regarding its purpose or what lesson I was supposed to learn. I finally asked the Father about the significance of this incredibly beautiful egg. He said it represented all the different facets of Him, and He was going to teach me about all of these facets. I continued to hold on to it for some time caressing it in my hands.

One evening Jesus came and asked me if I would like to see a facet of the crystal gold egg. "Oh yes!" was my excited response. He took my hand and we started walking down a staircase. The staircase passed through the sky and when we reached the bottom step, we sat down and looked over the city of Redding. In this vision the tops of the houses were gone and I could actually see into the homes. In some of the homes people were yelling at each other, while in others people were taking drugs. It seemed as though these homes held such despair, anger, hatred, and every guise of evil.

As I watched the people, Jesus sat beside me, but He remained silent. I looked at Him and there were tears running down His face. He spoke to the universe, "I love them. *I love them!* Who will tell them about Me? Who will tell them?" I told Him that I couldn't do it because I trip over my words and most of the things I do say come out wrong. Jesus knew I had always identified with Moses being slow of speech. But He said, "If you just open your mouth, the Holy Spirit will speak through you to tell them of Me." He turned His head and continued watching the people in their homes with no roofs. Tears were now dripping in great drops from His chin. I started to cry. I reached up and wiped away His tears and told Him that I would open my mouth. I would let the Holy Spirit speak through me so they could hear about Him.

I meditated for a moment on what had just taken place. I saw Jesus' intense love for the lost, His tears of pain for them and His command to go and tell them that He loves them. And right then Jesus asked me if I wanted to see another facet of the golden crystal egg.

The Warrior

Suddenly, Jesus transported me to another place. No longer were we in the sky, but my feet were on the ground once again in God's city. Standing beside Jesus was a magnificent white horse in full battle garb. Jesus mounted the horse. Behind Him was a multitude of warrior angels all decked out in armor. They started marching in place. The sound was thunderous, shaking the ground where I stood. Jesus looked down at me and pointed to the Father. I ran over to my Father and climbed onto His lap. I stood on His legs with my back against His chest while His arms held me steadily against Him. I watched with excitement as my most wonderful Bridegroom turned to His troops and motioned them onward. The ground rolled back and below I saw what appeared to be a beehive surrounded by swarming bees. Jesus gave the command and the warriors started to march with Jesus in front. As they began marching, the bees increased their activity, and when Jesus and the troops drew closer, the bees began to part and expose their hive.

Then I saw that it wasn't a beehive at all; it was the earth. And what looked like bees were actually demonic beings holding the earth captive. They began fleeing from the coming King and His army of angel warriors.

I noticed a particularly large group of demonic beings in a tight group. When Jesus rode up to them, they parted to expose the father of lies—satan himself. Jesus rode near, leaned over the side of His horse, and grabbed satan by the scruff of the neck with His right hand. He then lifted satan up and over the horse's neck and threw him down into a pit, which was on His right side. The lid of the pit was like a manhole cover, and it was promptly slammed shut. Then a great lock was put in place to keep the lid closed. Jesus started to march again, and as He neared the earth, the people there who had been watching the battle above them let out an enormous shout of praise.

I was deliriously excited. I turned to the Father and asked, "May I go down there?" He released me from His arms and instantly I was among the throngs of people on earth. There were people from every nation and yet we were all speaking the same language. We were rejoicing, shouting, "Hosanna, hosanna, the King has come, the King has come; holy and mighty is our King Jesus." Jesus was marching down the street and I was so proud. There was my King, my Betrothed, and my Love. When He came by me, He stopped and smiled. Oh how wonderful He is!

The Fragrance of His Love

After this I found myself again standing with Jesus holding the crystal gold egg in one hand and covering it with the other, cupping it in a protective way. I didn't know what to do with this object. I certainly didn't want to put it down. My pockets were too filled with the fragrance of Jesus' love. So I asked Jesus what I should do with this lesson. He told me to wear it around my neck. I lifted my hand to look at the egg and saw a fine golden chain attached to it. I lovingly put it over my head and took notice that the chain was long enough so that the egg was positioned right over my heart. Was this not the answer to my prayer to know the heart of God? Now the nature of God and the fragrance of His pure love lay forever near my heart.

CHAPTER 15

SECRET LOVE

I had my arms around my Father's neck and my lips next to His ear telling Him how much I loved Him. This is my favorite position because when my mouth is next to His ear, our faces are touching and the intimacy of the moment is almost over-powering to me. He told me to sit down, so I sat on His lap. Jesus came close, and resting my head on my Father's chest and taking Jesus' hand in mine, I closed my eyes. The world in all its grandeur could not come close to equaling the glory of His love and peace that was in my heart at that moment.

I opened my eyes and I saw Jesus staring intently at me. I caught my breath—I had seen that expression before. I had worn that expression before, and I knew exactly the kind of love it took to make that expression happen on a face. When my children were born, I would hold them in my arms and stare at them, and so tenderly I would touch their little faces. How wonderful they were; how I marveled at the lives God had allowed me to create. As they grew, that feeling never changed. Even now, though they are in their adult years, they will catch me staring at them. I do that because they are still so full of wonder to me. I still marvel at the miracle that brought them to me. That was the expression that Jesus had on His face. He was marveling at His creation; He was marveling at me. Even though we have made wrong decisions and hurt Him, He marvels at the wonder of His creation.

My oldest son, Jon, was not known for being very demonstrative. I knew he felt things deeply, but he didn't let his feelings show externally. If I told him I loved him, his reply would be "Yeah." One Mother's Day when he was in high school he came to me and told me he didn't have any money to purchase a gift, but he wanted to give me something. Then he wrapped his arms around me, kissed me on the cheek, and told me he loved me very much. Well, there is no material gift that could have meant more to me. No gift he could purchase could surpass what he had just done. We love to hear such words from the ones we love. How much more does our Father want to hear those words from us?

As I was thinking about that kind of love, I remembered how my children, when they were very young, ran to me for comfort when they had hurt themselves. I hugged and kissed them and softly spoke the "there-there" words, assuring them they were going to be OK. Soon they skipped away to play once more, with no thought for the pain that just minutes before had been so consuming. If I am totally honest, in a tiny corner of my heart I had just a little bit of joy when they were hurt. How could I have joy in their pain? It's not because I wanted them to hurt, but because they ran to me and I got to hold them and kiss away the pain and be their source of comfort.

This is how it worked for me. I don't know exactly how it works in the heart of a perfect God. But I know He has joy when we come running to Him when we hurt. I wonder if our comforter, our wonderful Holy Spirit, smiles just a tad because He hopes we will allow Him to wrap His arms around us and kiss our hurts. I said to Him, "My Lord, is this yet another facet? As a parent longs for her children to come to her so she can love them and comfort them, do You also long earnestly for us to come to You at all times for the benefits of Your tender love? Lord, I don't ever want to become self-sufficient and independent from Your dealings in my life. I want to live my life in Your arms and never move away from the loving 'there-there' words of comfort, the healing tender touches and the truth that is in Your presence." He always seems to be pleased when I catch on to what He's revealing to me.

Emotional Healing

One night while I was at a Randy Clark meeting, I went forward when a call went out for those who wanted a healing anointing. There was a press of people and I could feel the presence of God so strongly that I knew I wouldn't be able to stand much longer. I found a place to quietly lie down, and Jesus came to me and asked me if I wanted to see something. Oh yes!

Jesus took me to a place where a large portal opened in front of me. Behind the portal I could see a beautiful garden. Starting at the left side of the portal, my eyes moved right as I took in the sight of this beautiful garden, and there on the right I saw my earthly dad standing in the garden. I was so stunned I gasped, "You're here!" My dad said, "Yes, I just made it." If anyone had told me he would be in Heaven I would not have believed it possible. He had had an aortic aneurysm, and because he did not want to live anymore, he had done nothing about it. His neighbor had mentioned that about three days before he died, my dad felt his aneurysm was about to burst. During that time he must have asked Jesus to be his Savior.

My mind was reeling. Although I tried to move over toward him, it was as though my feet were glued to the ground. And he was not able to come to where I was standing. Then he said, "I'm so sorry." I knew he was sorry for all of the hurt he had caused in my life. I didn't know what to do, as I could hardly take it in. I started to turn around but he called my name and said, "I want you to know I think you're beautiful. I love you and I am so proud of you." Wow. Just like that, he had said what every little girl longs for her daddy to say. Then the portal closed. My mind was reeling. What had just happened?

I looked to my right where Jesus was standing and there beside Him was my grandmother. This was the grandmother who had told me I could never do anything right. She came over to me, laid her right hand on my face, and said, "I'm sorry."

Oh the healing that took place in those moments! I felt tremendous relief and joy that my earthly father will be waiting for me. Of course, Jesus did not have to show me this now.

I could have discovered it all later, when I went to Heaven permanently after leaving this earth. But in my Father's loving-kindness, He chose to heal a huge part of me "early."

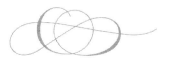

CHAPTER 16

THE CROSS OF LOVE AND OBEDIENCE

Jesus came to me one day and asked me if I wanted to see another facet. He took my hand and we began to travel extremely fast. Everything passed by me in a blur, and I knew we were moving very fast because my clothes were pressed against me as though I were standing in front of a high velocity fan. My hair was flying straight out behind me and I could feel the skin on my face being pulled back by the force. I asked Jesus where we were going and He said we were going back in time.

Once we stopped, I saw Jesus as He was about to be whipped before His crucifixion. I turned to Him and hid my face in His waist. I told Him I could not, would not, watch this. He put His arms around me and said, "You must. You must. For if it weren't for this, you would not be in My arms right now. If it weren't for this, you wouldn't have fellowship with our Father, and if it weren't for this you wouldn't have the Spirit of the living God dwelling within you. You must. You must see it." So I turned my head and watched but stayed right there in His arms.

The first lash hit its mark. As the blood began to flow I cringed. I saw the Father start to rise from His throne and I heard the heart of Jesus saying, "No, Father, no. They don't know what they are doing. Forgive them." The second lash came and again the Father started to rise. "No, Father, forgive them." The third, fourth, and fifth lashes came, and again He cried out for the Father to forgive. The 10th, 15th, 20th, 30th, and 39th lashes came, and after each one the cry of our Savior was, "Forgive them, Father, forgive them. They don't know what they are doing." I was nearly convulsed with tears in my vision, and I was physically aware of tears running down my cheeks.

Then I watched Him carry the cross. He stumbled, and the Simon the Cyrene came up to carry it for Him. Do you know what His heart cried out? He cried out, "Thank You, Father. Thank you for sending Me help." He was thankful and did not hesitate to say so to His Father. Through the pain and suffering, He thanked His Father for this seemingly small gesture of help as He continued on His course to Golgotha. He continued asking for the Father to forgive us until the end. Then He cried it aloud from the cross, "Forgive them, Father, for they know not what they do."

After this we made our way back through time to the throne room. As I stood crying in front of Him, He said, "There is forgiveness for both the saved and the unsaved, but it only comes through Me and you must receive it. It's there for you always. The Almighty God is a God of forgiveness. There will be people who go to eternal separation from Us because they did not come to the Father's forgiveness. There are people who, when they come to eternal fellowship with Us, will wonder why they didn't receive the forgiveness that came through Me and live in that forgiveness."

I came to realize that the forgiveness we receive through Jesus is complete. There are no cracks or holes in it; no strings attached. It is there for the asking. People need to know this. We believers have to tell them.

The Crystal Cube

The Holy Spirit took me to another pedestal, upon which sat an object like a glass or crystal cube, about the size of a Rubik's Cube. The Spirit said that this cube represented obedience. He told me to hold it tight, so I squeezed and held onto the cube tightly. Because the cube had corners it wasn't as comfortable to hold as a round object, but I could do it. Then He told me to hold it cock-eyed. When I turned it as He directed, the corners were pressed directly into my palms. He told me to hold it tightly. So I squeezed it as hard as I could, holding tightly, but this time it hurt. The points were digging into my palms. It hurt so much that I threw it to the ground and it shattered.

I quickly looked at the Holy Spirit—I couldn't believe that I had broken the cube. I was wide-eyed as I looked at Him to see if He was angry. He wasn't. He smiled at me and said, "There is a right way to handle obedience and a wrong way. When held tightly and done correctly, obedience can be uncomfortable, but you can do it. If you are obedient but have anger or resentment at having to do something that is asked of you, you will start to complain and murmur about the tasks. There will be no peace or joy in following My instructions, and because of that, the pain of obedience will be so great that you will throw it from you. Remember, Jesus endured the cross for the joy set before Him. Always look past the obedience to the joy. Never will anything be asked of you that great joy will not come from it. Hold obedience correctly."

He then bent down and picked up a small sliver of the broken cube. He took my hand and embedded the sliver into the palm of my hand. It hurt and I started to withdraw my hand, but I decided that I would endure the pain for the joy of remembering how He cares enough to be my Teacher. He then handed me another cube and told me to place it on my forehead and push. When I pushed the cube against my forehead, the cube went into my head.

The sliver is to remind me of what happens when I handle obedience incorrectly, and the cube is to remind me to be obedient for the joy set before me.

CHAPTER 17

EVEN MORE OBJECT LESSONS

Light of the World

Another day the Holy Spirit took me to a pedestal that had an object on it about the size of a small bead. I gingerly picked it up between my thumb and forefinger and asked Him what it was. Before the Holy Spirit could answer me, a great light burst forth from the bead. It was so bright that I could not see. I covered it quickly with my other hand to protect my eyes and again asked Holy Spirit what it was. He told me it represented the Light of the World—Jesus. I was told to put it in my eye.

When I did so, I immediately found myself standing on the shore of a harbor. I was a lighthouse. Out of my eye shined the Light of the World. Ships were coming into this safe harbor, but there were many obstructions in the way: barrier reefs, rocks, sand bars, flotsam, and every sort of danger that could cause harm or destruction. I knew my job was to watch the ships as they came into the harbor, lighting up the obstructions, helping them to find safe passage. The ships were coming into this safe harbor at different speeds.

I knew the lesson almost instantly. We believers are the lighthouses—we have the light. It is important that we show people the way and warn them of the impediments and obstructions that can sink them before reaching safety. We aren't foghorns blowing that dreadful sound; we are lighthouses lighting the way, exposing the snares, and allowing people to see the way. We must not allow our light to dim and we must always have enough fuel on hand to keep the light burning brightly. We must never allow ourselves to think that we have plenty of fuel and need no more, or that we can wait to get more fuel after a particular storm has passed. We cannot allow ourselves ever to burn out!

Faith

I walked over to the next pedestal, but it was empty. I leaned over and looked closer, but I could see absolutely nothing on that pedestal. Almost in frustration I said to the Holy Spirit, "There's nothing here." He responded by saying that yes, there was and that I just needed to look more closely. After staring intently, without blinking my eyes, I still saw nothing. He smiled and said it was faith there on the pedestal and that I should scoop it up with my hands. He then told me to put it on my feet like a pair of slippers. Ah yes, faith—the essence of things unseen.

It was curious to me that He told me to put faith on like slippers. Why not shoes or boots or sneakers? "Slippers are comfortable," He explained. "They are what you put on after a long day; they are warm and comforting." I came to understand that I should be so comfortable with my faith that I could walk into any situation knowing that the Holy Spirit would instruct and direct me. This did not mean that I could take faith for granted. It just meant that I needed to be comfortable with the measure of faith God had given me while increasing my faith every day.

The Bar

After the measure of faith, I was led to another pedestal. Lying on it was a bar. When I picked it up I immediately saw a runner running a race with a baton in his hand. The Holy Spirit confirmed that the bar signified running a race. Endurance in a race will get you to the end of the course. I broke the baton into two pieces and placed them along my shins. The pieces will remind me to run the race, enduring until the end.

Later at home I sat at my desk and I looked up the word *endure* in the thesaurus. Some of its synonyms are: *abide, continue, persist, remain,* and *outlast.* I looked at my ankles and in the spirit could see the broken baton pieces. I knew that I could persist and outlast.

The Staff

One day I was with my Father, just loving Him and enjoying His love, when He set me down in front of Him, took a crown, and put it on my head. Then He handed me a staff. The definition of *staff* is "used as support in walking or climbing, or as a weapon; a rod carried as a symbol of authority."[1] I felt that all three of these dimensions were signified in the staff my Father had given me. I carry with me a symbol of authority as a member of the Royal Family. I have the support of my Family as I travel through my adventures with Them. And I have the ultimate weapon against the evil one—the King Himself.

Endnote

1. "staff." *Microsoft Word Dictionary.* 2008, Mac version 12.2.6.

CHAPTER 18

Intimately His

We were standing in the place that held the objects and the pedestals and I had my arms around the Father's neck. He took me by the shoulders and moved me back so there was a foot or so of space between us. His glory radiated from Him in splendid streams that were so beautiful to see. He put His hand to His chest and "pinched" out a little bit of His glory—sort of like a "starter" (like yeast for making bread)—and reached over and put it in me. I started to laugh, a joy-filled laugh. I had some glory. I had some glory! Oh glory, I had some glory! I ran over to Jesus and showed Him that I had some of His glory in me. He was so happy. When we're happy with what He has given us and done for us, the Father, Jesus, and the Holy Spirit are happy too.

The Holy Spirit came over and asked me for a dance. Always before when I had danced with Him, my feet had stayed on the ground while He soared around, seemingly unhampered by the gravity that held me to the floor. This time He took me in His arms and we both soared up and away in a marvelous dance. I was laughing and He was smiling at me. Then He leaned over to me and said, "I love you."

I replied, "I also love Him."

He then said, "I love the Father,"

"Oh yes," I said, "I do too."

Then He said, "I love Jesus."

"I do too."

He leaned over again and said that we were practicing for the day when the Bride and the Bridegroom would dance at Their wedding. He was teaching me how to be sensitive to His leading, how at His slightest move or suggestion I would be able to follow Him. I love dancing with the Spirit. I simply cannot wait until my wedding day when I will dance with my Jesus. Apparently, the Lord cannot wait for the wedding day either. For He gave me a glimpse of what is to come. And I want to share it with you.

The Wedding

I stood at the door of a cathedral, impressive in size and splendid in appearance. I looked in the doorway and I saw my Father standing way down at the front of the aisle. To His side stood Jesus with His head bowed. The rows upon rows of seats were transparent like purest glass, and they were full of the heavenly hosts, dressed in gossamer robes. These heavenly hosts were extremely excited, filling the atmosphere with an incredible anticipation that was actually tangible to my senses.

As I stood in the doorway, trumpets sounded, brilliant in tone and volume, heralding this majestic moment. Then the Holy Spirit pushed the doors open and offered His arm to the Bride. As soon as I stepped through the doorway, it was not just me but the entire Bride of Christ walking down the aisle. My Father smiled, the heavenly hosts stopped their excited whispering and turned to watch, and then Jesus' head came up. Oh, if you could have seen His response to the sight of His beautiful Bride! His smile was radiant, expressing His great joy for that long-awaited day.

Jesus started toward His Bride, but the smiling Father reached over and touched His arm, holding Him back. Jesus had already come for the Bride. Now it was the Bride's turn to come to Jesus. He stood there, still and poised, as the Holy Spirit walked the Bride down that seemingly long aisle. Jesus never took His eyes off His Bride. When the Spirit and the Bride neared the altar of God, they stopped. The Father reached out and took the hand of the Bride and placed it in the hand of His Son. He then said, "Jesus, I present Your Bride without spot or wrinkle."

All of Heaven rejoiced. Multitudes of angelic beings started to worship and the Bride joined them in adoration of her wonderful Bridegroom—her Beloved.

Thoughts

After this last vision of the wedding to come, I began to think that this was the end of the visions—and what an end! In a way, I was hoping that it was the end. These visions were wonderful. The time I spent with my God, my Jesus, and my Holy Spirit was incredibly sweet—like a vision within a vision. I don't consider my time just talking with Them to be in the same dimension as my visions, but I guess it really is. Or is it? It is so real—I *feel* Jesus' arms around me. I *hear* my Father whisper in my ear, and I *feel* my Holy Spirit as He dances around me. But it isn't happening in the natural dimension, even though it truly feels as though it is real. Sometimes the fabric that divides the natural realm from the spirit realm is so sheer and permeable that you can reach through it with your hand or accidentally bump into this realm unexpectedly.

CHAPTER 19

HEARTS

Earlier I neglected to tell you about the window I saw when I was among the pedestals and their objects. I noticed the window at the back of the room and was given permission to go look out and see what was there. The window was made of opaque glass, so I had to push it open in order to see what was outside. Through the open window I saw an astonishingly beautiful park. The stream that came from God's throne also ran through the garden, somehow turning back as it flowed through this park outside the window. However, the stream was wider and much deeper here than it was in the garden—it was a river. In fact, this park greatly resembled the garden, only it was quite a bit larger—it seemed to go on as far as my eyes could see. From my viewpoint in the window I was much higher than the park. As I looked out, I saw someone standing by a grove of trees, but I couldn't see who it was.

I was thinking about all of this when Jesus came and asked me if I wanted to see another facet of the crystal gold egg. After I tell you about it, I'll come back and tell you the rest of what happened in the park.

Where's My Heart?

Once again I was standing in front of Jesus as a little girl. He took His heart and gave it to me. We walked for a while, and I was very careful as I held this precious heart. Then I found myself standing in a kitchen and Jesus was no longer there. I heard children playing outside, but I couldn't go out to play because I was holding Jesus' heart. I wanted to go outside and play so much that I carefully put His heart on the table and ran out to play. After a short while I found Jesus standing next to me. I looked up and He leaned over and kindly asked, "Where is My heart?" I thought, *Uh-oh*. I ran into the house and picked up His heart and thought, I'll never put His heart down again.

Then I saw some cookies on a shelf. I walked over to the shelf and reached up with one hand to get the cookies, holding His heart in my other hand because I didn't want to set His heart down again. Unfortunately, I couldn't quite reach the cookies with one hand, so I tucked His heart under my chin and lowered my head to hold it, freeing my hands to get the cookies. The heart slipped out and fell to the floor. Jesus was there in that instant and He bent over, picked up His heart, took it over to the sink, and washed it off. Again He gave His heart back to me. I thought to myself, *I'll never put His heart under my chin again. Hearts seem to be slippery.*

Then I decided to go for a walk. As I walked, His heart jiggled in my hands and it was kind of fun. So I started stomping as I walked to make it jiggle more. Then I started tossing Jesus' heart in the air gently, eventually juggling the heart from one hand to the other. Unfortunately, I missed a toss and His heart landed on the ground. At that point the vision ended, but I understood completely what Jesus was teaching me.

How often do we set His heart aside to "do our own thing"? When we go our own way we often leave Jesus' heart behind. And when we want fleshly gratification we tend to become careless with His heart. In our daily lives we often neglect to give His heart the respect and honor it deserves. I also realized that when I put His heart aside, became careless with it, or didn't give it the honor I should have, Jesus was never mad. I knew He was sad, but never mad, and He always gave His heart back to me. Ahhh, I love this facet of God. He works with us over and over and over again to teach us how to hold His heart correctly and then how to love Him above our selfish desires and carelessness. Then He even gives a wonderful forgiveness for the times when we don't get it right. So now I try to always walk with His heart next to mine. I want to feel His heart beat for me and for all the other people.

The Window

Remember the window I told you about earlier that looked out over the park? The Holy Spirit came to me at the window and asked me if I would like to go to the park, which of course I did. Near the pedestals was a path and He led me down the path to the park. However, partway down the hill the path became very rocky. The rocks were big and it looked as though it would be easy to step from one rock to another, but I was not steady on my feet and was afraid of falling. The Holy Spirit told me to put my foot wherever He said and to hold onto His hand. He helped me like this—hand in hand—all the way down the hill. He is my Guide and my Comforter.

When we reached the bottom, we started to walk over to the trees where I had seen someone standing, and I realized that Jesus and my Father were both there. I ran to Them with outstretched arms giving Them both a hug. As soon as the Holy Spirit caught up with us, Jesus showed me a round table with chairs and told me to sit down. We all sat down—Jesus, the Father, the Holy Spirit, and me. Jesus looked at me and said, "I want you to put your heart on the table." I really didn't like the way that sounded, but I knew I didn't have anything to fear. So I put my heart there on the table before Jesus and the Holy Spirit. I got up and walked away, leaving my heart on the table. Somehow I just knew I needed to leave Them and not go back until They called for me. I waited nearby, but out of hearing range. The next day They were still talking! I wanted desperately to know what They were saying, but I knew I had to wait.

Isn't the mind a wonderful and terrible thing? The thought came to me that They were probably discussing how black my heart was and that They wouldn't be able to use it. I didn't really believe this lie, because even if my heart was too black, even if it was a lump of coal, I knew They would make it healthy or give me a new one. I love Them so much. Then I became anxious, in a good way, to know what was coming next.

I have discovered that when the Father, Son, and Holy Spirit are taking me through a process in a vision that extends over a few days, I can still meet with Them in another place to talk. In the middle of this vision where They were working on my heart, I met with the Holy Spirit and asked Him to teach me more quickly. I wanted everything to go faster. He laughed and said that He was waltzing while I wanted to do the jitterbug. If I wanted to dance with the Holy Spirit, I needed to know how He was dancing and fall into step with Him. Otherwise I would be doing my own thing, in my own strength, and without the grace that comes from following His lead.

Eventually Jesus nodded to me and I walked back to the table. I watched as Jesus picked up my heart. He took a little patch of His heart, put it on my heart, and sewed it in place. Then He handed it to the Holy Spirit, who also took a piece of His heart and sewed it to my heart. The Holy Spirit handed my heart to the Father and He also took a patch of His heart and sewed it to mine. Then Jesus handed my patchwork heart back to me. The Father said that Their heart was really one heart, beating with the same beat, but He had shown me this picture of all three of Them giving me a piece of Their heart because He wanted me to know that these pieces were to be nurtured and allowed to grow until they totally consumed my heart.

CHAPTER 20

Having Fun in the Garden

Sitting Around the Campfire

One day I walked over to the river that was in the garden. This was the river of God's glory, which had become so familiar to me. I sat down and put my feet into the water. Then my Father walked over and sat down next to me. As I looked down I noticed that in my hand I had a very simple fishing pole and the line was in the water. I was actually fishing in the river, and it was so much fun. My Father asked me what I was fishing for. I thought about that for just a moment, and with a big smile on my face, I looked up at Him and said, "Men." He laughed out loud at that and said, "Good." He asked me what I was using for bait. I thought for a moment, and again, with another big smile on my face I said very slowly, "Love." He put

His arm around me, pulled me to Him and said, "That is very good. The more bait you use, the more you will catch."

Another time I found myself walking back to a table where Jesus and the Holy Spirit were sitting. Jesus asked me if I would like to go somewhere with Him. We started to walk and we came upon my Father, who was sitting in a small clearing by a campfire. There were logs in the fire and the flames were hungrily crackling and snapping at them. We all sat there in companionable silence, listening to the logs being devoured.

After a while the fire grew much warmer, as though someone had turned the thermostat way up. I became so uncomfortable that I had to walk away from the heat. As I turned and looked back toward the campfire, I saw all three of Them sitting there with Their heads down. I knew I had done something wrong, so I quickly walked back to the Father and asked what I had done. He said that it was His fire and some-times it would grow very warm and become uncomfortable, but that I should never leave, not even for a short time—not unless I was told to do so. He said that others had left, and still others would leave, because sometimes the fire is just too uncomfortable. Then He said that those who had left the fire were out in the woods shivering. While they could see the fire, some were fearful of coming back, some were too prideful, and some just didn't think they needed His fire.

I turned around and saw someone standing at the edge of the clearing. Indeed this person was shivering and appeared very cold and scared but yearning to be by the Father. I looked at the Father and asked Him if this person was one of the ones whom He had been talking about. "Yes, she is," He replied.

He told me to get some fire. So I stuck my bare hand into the fire and pulled out a single flame about the size of a plum. I held the flame in the palm of my hand. Then He told me to go and give the fire to this person. I took it over to her and hugged her, holding her until I could feel her warming with love from the embrace. I stood back and gave her my little flame. I knew that she would go back to the fire and sit with the Father, Jesus, and the Holy Spirit.

I quickly returned to the fire and asked the Father to turn the fire into a blaze. As for me, I wanted to stand in the fire and let it consume me. I understood that if being this close was uncomfortable at times, then standing in the fire would be extremely uncomfortable. But the way I figured it, that's where we should be, in the middle of God's fire, white-hot for Him.

I started dancing and spinning through the fire. I actually twirled right through my Father, Jesus, and the Holy Spirit while They laughed.

The List

One day the Father led me over to another clearing where I saw a table. He took out a paper and spread it across the table. Then He said that it was a list of all the things He wanted me to do and He asked me if I could do them. I read the list, which included things like share my Jesus with others, help to set the captives free, speak with love to all people, show the grace of my Father, etc. The list was in three columns and it was in very fine print. I told Him I didn't know if I could do it.

You see, I was willing, but I didn't know if I could actually do all that was on the list.

He called the Holy Spirit to come and stand at my right side. My Father asked the Holy Spirit, "Can You do all these things?"

The Holy Spirit smiled and quickly looked over the list. He said, "Oh yes, I can do all of this."

My Father put His right hand on my left shoulder, His left hand on the Holy Spirit's right shoulder, and gently started to push. The Holy Spirit and I became as one. I was aware that He was filling up all of me. My Father asked Him again, "Can you do all of these things?"

The Holy Spirit smiled again and said, "Yes, I can do all those things."

It tickled me when He spoke and I started to giggle. Then He started to giggle and the Father just smiled and waited for us to stop. Then my Father asked me again, "Can you do all of these things?"

"Oh yes," I replied, "With my wonderful Helper, I can do all of these things."

You see, He didn't ask if I could do all of them without ever making a mistake. He just asked if I could do them. Does He want me to do them without a mistake? Oh yes, but He also knows that it will take practice and He's so patient, kind, and forgiving of my mistakes. So I don't ever have to fear making mistakes, and I can do all things through Christ Jesus who strengthens me and by the Holy Spirit who dwells in me.

Learning to Dance

Then the Holy Spirit and I started to dance again, and this time I wasn't just standing while He danced around me. This dance wasn't the soaring dance we had done previously but a deliberate step-by-step dance of me learning to follow His lead—learning the gentle pressure of His hand on my back and the subtle movement of His hand in mine. I knew it was to become the dance of two people who had danced a thousand dances together; a couple who had learned to detect even the slightest of nuances from their partner and was able to anticipate a change in direction even before the rhythm became apparent.

After we had finished dancing we came back to the table, and my wonderful Father called Jesus over to where we were standing. He said, "My Son, describe My daughter to Me." And then the Father closed His eyes.

Jesus looked over at me, smiled, and said, "Well, she loves Us very much. She tries very hard and she hates it when she sins. Remember the time she...." He went on to describe the times I had been in a test or a trial and had run to Them for help. Jesus went on and on about me.

I realized that He never once described my hair, eyes, height, weight, or color. And He never once said anything negative about me—and He certainly could have. He was describing **me.** Not the me that I don't like or the me that had not conquered a particular sin, but the *me* that He saw.

When Jesus was done, the Father opened His eyes and said to me, "I have just seen you through the eyes of love."

Doesn't He see all of us that way? Aren't we funny people not to run to Him for everything because we are afraid He will see the bad? He only sees us through the eyes of the love of our wonderful and majestic Lord Jesus.

Gulliver

Another day Jesus took my hand and we started walking through the woods. We went down some steps and we came to a small village. Now when I say a "small village" I mean a miniature toy village, complete with thatched roof cottages like an old-fashioned English village. There were little businesses on the main street and a lot of little people were going about their business.

There, in the middle of the town square, was the Holy Spirit. He was lying on the ground and He was all trussed up with little ropes the people had put there to keep Him bound. He looked just like Gulliver from Jonathan Swift's *Gulliver's Travels.* He had a big smile on His face as He lifted one hand up, making the ropes snap and fall off as though they were only cotton string. The people scrambled to fix all of the ropes and tie Him down again. I heard the people saying. "Oh no, oh no! He's loose! We've got to tie Him down again." Then He did the same thing with the other hand and the people began running around, trying to tie Him up again.

Finally He stood up and broke the ropes, easily shaking them off. He squatted down and said to the people, "Hello. I'm the Holy Spirit and I'm not going to let you tie Me up anymore."

I laughed so hard. Isn't that what we "little people" do? We think we can tie up the Holy Spirit and keep Him in control. Now that's a laugh!

Inside the Heart of the Father

Then Jesus, the Holy Spirit, and I started walking back up the steps hand in hand. We walked for a while and I noticed that I couldn't see the Father. I asked Jesus where He was and Jesus told me to turn around. I looked behind me and there He was. He was *huge!* I started to climb up in His lap and continued to climb up His chest, eventually resting in a fold of His garment. I could tell I was next to His heart because I could hear it beating. "Ka-love, ka-love, ka-love" sounded in my ear. Then I slept for a while because I was so tired from climbing such a great distance.

When I awoke, the Father put His right hand up to me and I climbed up onto His hand. Now I realize that the next part of this sounds very strange, but I am writing just as I saw it. The Father tossed me into His mouth like a pill and swallowed me! Traveling fast, I ended up in His heart. I was standing to one side, watching as cells rushed in and out of His heart like waves. Each cell was labeled: *LOVE.* I looked across His heart and saw people I knew. I waved at them and they waved back. I even saw my two sons. They were in the recesses of His heart, in the shadows, for they were not walking with God at that time. They weren't joining in our joy at being in the heart of God. They were very stiff, but they were there. Everyone is in God's heart because He loves everyone, but not everyone joins in and those who don't join in have no joy.

I became concerned when I didn't see Pastor Bill and Beni. *Maybe this isn't of the Lord,* I wondered. But just then, Pastor Bill and Beni rode in on one of the love cell waves. They rode the love cells like you would ride a horse and Pastor Bill was even wearing a cowboy hat. They had been looking around, and they told me and some other friends to come with them so they could show us what they had seen. Each of us jumped on a love cell and began to follow them. They led us by God's throat so we could hear what His voice sounded like. Then we went up to His eyes where we stopped. Here we could walk up to His eyes and look out, like we were in an observation tower.

As I looked out through His eyes, I thought, *Well, would you look at that. The harvest indeed is ripe and ready to be gathered. There are some workers out there but not nearly enough. Some of those who are being harvested right now are going to become harvesters themselves.*

Then we got back on our love cells and headed for the Father's brain. His brain had electrical charges that were going through all of the synapses. Each electrical charge was like a pink neon sign that flashed: *LOVE.* Hundreds of thousands of pink flashes of *LOVE* going off and on—it was an incredible light show.

Next we went on down to His hands where we could see how He does things. Then we all headed for His feet so we could see where He was going. Lastly, we went back to His heart.

When He swallowed me I wasn't afraid because I knew He wouldn't chew me up or spit me out.

CHAPTER 21

FINDING YOUR WAY BACK TO INTIMACY

The Jungle

Next, I found myself back in the garden with my Father, Jesus, and the Holy Spirit. They were talking and I didn't understand what They were saying, so I got a little bored. I noticed a jungle-like area that was nearby and it had a path going to it, so I decided to explore. After a while the path became darker as all of the trees, vines, and plants became very dense. Then I came to a clearing. All of a sudden, a saber-toothed tiger jumped out at me, roaring with his teeth bared. I just stood there very still as the tiger continued to snarl.

I started to call for Jesus and the Holy Spirit, but just when I opened my mouth, the tiger snarled louder and moved toward me. I stopped. I was so scared that I just stood there, very still. I began to wonder, *How am I going to get myself out of this fix?* Then I reasoned that even if the tiger ate me I had nothing to fear. This jungle was in God's garden so I must be immune from danger. As I took a step to walk away, the tiger lunged at me, but I had a protective shield around me. The tiger hit the shield, bounced off, and then ran away. So I decided that I would just keep on walking deeper into the jungle.

Next, I ducked under a low-hanging branch, and on the branch was an enormous snake. The snake put his head right in front of me and started to hiss. The snake had a huge head—as big as mine. He could have swallowed me in one gulp. I stood very still. And again, as soon as I opened my mouth to call for help, the snake began to open its mouth and crept closer to my head. But I'd been through this same thing with the tiger, so I started to walk away. Just as with the tiger, the protective shield stopped the snake. He just bonked his head, bounced off the shield, then slithered away.

Then I came to a clearing and there was a person sitting there. At first, I thought it was my Jesus, so I ran to Him. I ran up and fell at His feet and put my head on His lap. But as soon as my head rested on His lap, I knew it wasn't Jesus. It was a stone person—a statue. I looked at the face of the statue and it had a stone tear on its stone cheek. I got up and tried to go back the way I had come, but I couldn't find the path. I did see another path, however, and as I ran down the path I came to a cave. As I approached the cave a huge black bear came ambling out on all fours. Once again, I knew what to do. I just turned around and ran back toward the clearing.

On the way back I stopped to sit on a log beside the path to catch my breath. *If only I had a map,* I thought, *I would be able to find my way out of this place.* At that moment I glanced down and saw a map lying in front of my feet. I quickly looked around. I knew someone had to have left it there just a few moments ago because it hadn't been there when I sat down. But I didn't see anyone at all in the immediate area. So I proceeded to open up the map and study it. The map showed the tiger place, the snake place, the clearing with the statue, the bear cave, and the path that would take me out of the jungle. After looking at the map, I realized that I needed to return to the clearing where the statue sat.

So I got up and took the path back to the clearing. When I came into the clearing, the statue came to life and began screeching at me. Then the statue stood up and started walking toward me. I knew that the statue wanted me to stay in the jungle, and I sensed that if it got to me, it would try to hold me back. The statue was going very slowly, lumbering from one heavy foot to the next. I was frightened, so I started to run toward the path that would take me out of that place, but my feet and legs felt like cement. Suddenly, I felt very tired. I kept going, but the more I struggled with my feet and legs, the more tired I got, and the desire to lie down was almost overwhelming. I started to pick up my legs with my hands—right, left, right, left—all the while the wailing statue was pursuing me.

Out of the Jungle

When I finally made it out of the jungle, my Father, Jesus, and the Holy Spirit were waiting for me. I ran to my Father, sat on His lap, and cried. I was so upset. Jesus came over and sat by us and wiped the tears from my cheeks. When I finally settled down, the Holy Spirit came over and held out His hand to me. I took His hand and He led me to a bench where we sat down.

I asked Him why all of this had happened. He answered, "You never asked Us about the jungle. You just took off on your own."

Then I asked about the statue, "Who did it represent and why did it chase me?"

He said it was someone who had gone into the jungle just like me but who had never made it out. I asked Him if He would have left me in there. He smiled and said, "Who do you think left you the map? I give a map to everyone, but some don't choose to look at it."

Back in the Jungle

Several days later, I was back at the same place in the jungle. I had been feeling sorry for the stone statue, so I asked the Father if I could go back and help the statue get out of the jungle. He answered, "Yes" and He put a huge, gold and silver sword in my hand. Across the blade was written *LOVE.*

Walking down the path into the jungle, I began to feel fearful and stopped about halfway. What if I got caught in the jungle again and couldn't get out? Then the Holy Spirit, who I didn't know was following me, leaned over my shoulder and whispered in my ear, "This time you were sent, and I'm going with you." This immediately gave me confidence and I entered the clearing boldly because I knew the Holy Spirit was with me.

When the statue saw me, it stood up and began to wail again as it came toward me. I raised the sword over my head, and when the statue came close, I plunged the sword into its heart. The statue immediately stopped, dead still. Then a chunk of stone fell off of its cheek and I could see flesh underneath. Soon other pieces of stone began to fall off, and underneath was a woman. I pointed to the path that would lead her out of the jungle and told her, "Run, run quickly. Get out!" Then I watched as she ran into the arms of the Father and Jesus. I was so happy I had helped to set a captive free.

Dancing With Me

Then out of the corner of my eye I could see movement. As I turned to look, I saw a whole bunch of statues coming toward me. I hadn't seen them before. Where had they been? I knew I couldn't handle all of them, and I began to feel fearful again. At that moment the Holy Spirit leaned over and said, "Dance with Me."

I thought to myself, *What? Dance? These statues are coming after me and He wants me to dance?*

He said it again, "Dance with Me."

So I thought, *OK, what do I have to lose?*

I still held the sword, only now His hand joined my hand on the sword. As we began to dance, the Holy Spirit positioned our steps so I could easily stab each statue in the heart. We danced around until we had stabbed all of the statues.

At one point, one of the statues almost grabbed me, but the Holy Spirit just twirled me out of harm's way and brought me around to stab the statue right in the heart. After each of the statues was stabbed, the stone fell off of it and the person underneath ran out of the jungle. Then the Holy Spirit and I walked out of the jungle as well.

As we came out of the jungle, I approached the first person who had been released from the stone and asked her why she and the others couldn't see that they had been turned into stone statues. She said that because the statues all looked alike they thought they were normal. When I came into the clearing they saw that I appeared quite different and it scared them. They wanted to grab me and make me just like them so I would stay and keep them company.

Sometime later I shared this particular vision with a friend. She later called me and said she felt like she was the statue. She wanted out but didn't know where her map was. Later, as I was praying for her, the Lord led me to a Scripture. Now I don't know what map you may need, but feel free to use the Scripture I gave my friend:

> *"For I know the plans that I have for you," declares the Lord, "plans for welfare and not for calamity to give you a future and a hope. Then you will call upon Me and come and pray to Me, and I will listen to you. You will seek Me and find Me when you search for Me with all your heart"* (Jeremiah 29:11-13).

The Orchard

Another day Jesus led me to an orchard that had trees loaded with fruit. Lying on the ground in the middle of this orchard was a red-and-white checkered tablecloth. Jesus told me to sit down on the tablecloth. Then He went over to a tree, picked a piece of fruit that looked similar to a peach, and brought it over to me. I had a small knife and I cut the fruit into four sections. Then I peeled each section from the seed and ate it. It was sweet and so good. When I had finished, He told me to cut open the pit. As I pried it open, a bug that looked like an earwig came out of the pit. This bug had eaten the seed that had been inside the pit.

Jesus told me that the bug had gotten into the pit without damaging the fruit, and no one even knew it was there. The fruit still tasted sweet, but the part of the fruit that could reproduce—the seed—had been destroyed. He told me to guard the seed with everything I had and to go to any lengths to see that the seed was not destroyed. I asked Him what the seed represented and He replied, "It is your love for Me." Are you wondering what the bugs represented? So was I. The bugs represented the snares of this world—things like anxiety, unforgiveness, and bitterness.

We sat there for a time just enjoying each other and our time together. Then a gentle wind started blowing, eventually getting stronger and stronger. I had not been aware of any weather in this place before, so I thought it strange. The wind continued to increase. I looked up at Jesus, but He seemed unconcerned. He saw my concern and pulled me up onto His lap. Fruit began to fall from the trees, but He still didn't seem concerned. Then I saw that it was the bad fruit that was falling and I felt better. I asked Him where the wind was coming from and He told me to look. I raised myself up and peeked over His shoulder. There at the edge of the orchard was my

Father—blowing. Jesus told me, "It is the breath of God. He is knocking the bad fruit off the trees so that the good fruit can grow bigger."

I had to laugh. I got up and started to run around the orchard in the breath of God. I was about four or five trees away from Jesus when I looked back and saw that He was standing and looking at me. I ran to Him and threw myself into His arms. He held me and we began to dance. Then He said, "I've heard you and the Holy Spirit have been practicing dancing for our wedding day. You only have to grow up a little more before you're ready."

I said, "Jesus, my Jesus, if I can do anything to hasten the day we can be together, please tell me. I long to be with You."

And He replied, "Just as I long to be with you."

CHAPTER 22

BLESSINGS AND OTHER GARDEN EXPERIENCES

One day my Father called Jesus over and asked Him to show me His storehouse. We crossed the river representing God's glory, and there I saw a huge storehouse. As we walked through the gigantic doors of this cavernous place, I saw enormous bins on each side of the building. Each bin had thousands upon thousands of blessings piled in it. Each blessing was represented by a ball about the size of an orange. These balls were all different colors and they represented all different kinds of blessings. There were financial blessings and healing blessings, including physical, emotional, mental, and spiritual healing. Joy and peace were in the bins—enough for everyone. I also noticed different gifts and talents piled high and far too numerous to list here. The colors were amazing and it seemed as though no blessing was quite the same color as another.

Each bin had a chute that poured the blessings onto a conveyor belt running through the middle of the building. This conveyor belt had built-up sides that were approximately 6 inches high. Blessings were all stacked up on the conveyor belt because the belt was not moving. I ran the entire distance to the end of the building to see where the belt was going. When I got to the end, there was a large opening in the building and from it a chute led down to the earth. I saw that a few of the blessings were falling off the end because the conveyor belt was so full, but a lot more blessings were just waiting there for the belt to start moving.

Jesus was standing at the same end of the building and had His hand on the switch that would turn on the motionless conveyor belt. I asked Him when He was going to turn it on, and He said, "As soon as the Father tells Me to." I ran out the door and over to my Father, crawled up onto His lap, and asked Him when He was going to tell Jesus to turn on the conveyor belt. He said, "Soon, very soon."

The Box

Another day we went back to the place where the Holy Spirit had shown me the creative objects and pedestals. He handed me a beautiful wooden cube that was about 4 inches by 4 inches and told me to open it. I looked and looked, but I couldn't find a place to open it. I looked up and said, "I can't open it."

He answered, "Yes, you can."

I continued to look for the opening of this box, running my fingers around the surface to see if there was a crack that I had missed. I finally became impatient. I looked at the box and spoke to it in frustration, "Oh open!" And it did. Now, I had thought that it would open at the edge of one side, but it opened right down the middle where there was no seam, just like an egg that cracks.

You'll have to think hard about what comes next because it's difficult to describe. The box opened and it had about a 2-inch lip around the sides. It looked like a box that had hinges in the middle of one side, but there were no hinges. What appeared to be inside was a piece of fuzz, which mystified me. Why would my Father keep a fuzz ball, or as my daughter would say, a "dust bunny," in this beautiful box?

I set the box down on the pedestal, and immediately each side that was standing up started to fold down. The sides kept unfolding more and more in every direction. The box began to get rather large and I thought it might knock over other things that were nearby. I stood in front of it and began to hold my hands out so it would grow in certain directions. The Father touched my shoulder, and when I looked up at Him, He said, "Don't stop it." He said it with wonder and excitement at what it was becoming. He didn't want me to get in the way of its growth and keep it from forming.

I stood by the Father and watched as it continued to unfold. I noticed that in the center that little dust ball was growing also. It was moving and bulging out in all directions. It reminded me of a Disney cartoon I had seen once of an atom with all the little ions going very fast around the nucleus. The edges of the box finally stopped folding down and I looked again at the fuzz ball. I was amazed to see that the tiny fuzz ball, which I had thought was just a dust bunny, had grown into a beautiful tropical garden with trees and plants and flowers. Wow, was it beautiful!

The Father took my hand and we flew up, over, and then down into the garden. As we passed one of the trees, the fronds brushed against my face. It was the softest, most gentle, most peaceful, most wonderful feeling—that a tree could feel like that was amazing!

We sat together, my Father and I, in this garden, and He started to talk to me about the box and the garden. He said that I must never stop His work. I had been so concerned that it would knock something over that I had been about to stop its progress. When He gives us something it may not look like much, and we might not be able to tell what it is, but if we just do as He says, it will open up for us. He went on to say that what He starts may not look very valuable or good to us (the fuzz ball), but He can take the littlest, most insignificant things and bring wonders out of them.

I remembered how people got very worried in the beginning of Toronto Blessing of 1994. The people were afraid of losing control. Perhaps some of their precious traditions (usually man-made ones) would be knocked over. Sometimes we see something that God starts as a "fuzz ball"—something of little value. Many people didn't think the joy and laughter were very valuable. But if we let God's plan (fuzz ball) unfold, it will grow into something that is of infinite value.

Galaxy in a Bottle

The Father took me again to His creation place. As I looked around, He told me, "You can go anywhere you want." I found a very interesting bottle on one of the pedestals. The bottle was shaped like a big gourd, about 1 foot tall, and appeared to be made of a moving opaque glass of beautiful blues and greens. When I tried to pick up the bottle it seemed too heavy to lift. So I told the Father I could not pick it up because it was too heavy. He told me, "Yes you can." So I tried again, but it still wouldn't budge.

I turned to the Father and again told Him it was too heavy. This time He said, "Yes you can. Just believe." I thought a moment and said to myself, *OK, I'm going to think of this as something that is as light as a feather.* As I reached out again to pick it up, it almost floated in my hands—just like a feather.

The lid of the bottle was very strange. It came off easily as though it were hinged, but I could not see any hinge or attachment to the bottle. I could roll the lid around the top lip of the bottle and it would come off, but it stuck to the bottle, almost like a magnet. I was fascinated with this and spent quite a bit of time just trying to figure out how the lid stayed attached to the bottle. After some time, I finally looked into the bottle and saw an incredible sight. Inside this bottle was an entire galaxy! It wasn't a picture or a model, but a real galaxy. As I peered inside the bottle I watched the galaxy rotate ever so slowly. What was so astounding was that the inside of the bottle was larger than the outside. The inside of the bottle went on forever. But when I looked at the outside of the bottle, it appeared as though it could hold very little. The whole thing was mind-boggling.

I began to wonder if the Father kept our galaxy in a bottle. So I turned and asked Him, as I pointed at the inside of the bottle, "Are there people in there?"

In a playful tone that parents use when our kids ask silly questions, He responded, "No, I don't keep My people in bottles."

Whew! Was I ever relieved to know that I'm not stuck in a bottle on some heavenly shelf! Then I asked Him if I could stick my finger in the bottle.

He said, "Nooooo." And I realized what might happen to all the planets and stars if I stuck my finger in that bottle and started moving things around.

The Scripture John 7:24 comes to mind, *"Do not judge according to appearance, but judge with righteous judgment."* You never want to make a judgment based on what something looks like on the outside, even a bottle!

Color My Garden

Our God loves gardens. He has a lot of them and enjoys showing them off to us. He has indeed created a garden for each of us to come to. A place of fellowship with Him, just as He walked with Adam and Eve in the Garden of Eden. I have seen so many different gardens in my journeys with Him. Each garden is a little different, and I learn a little more about Him in each place. I'll give you an example.

One day the Lord took me to a beautiful garden. There was a lovely creek that pooled into a pond surrounded by flowers. I could hear the water gently flowing over some rocks. This garden was very full of a variety of different flowers of all shapes and sizes, but interestingly enough the flowers were all in shades of lavender. As we sat there together gazing upon the beauty of the garden, I began to think about the color lavender. It's really not a color I'm drawn to in the natural. I don't dislike lavender, but I had always thought of it as being just a neutral color.

So then I began to wonder why the Lord had made this lavender garden for me. I was sure that He knew that my favorite color was red. As I was thinking this, He leaned over and said, "Would you like to see it in red?"

"Oh yes," I replied.

The flowers in the garden all instantly turned to different shades of red. My goodness! It looked like an explosion had gone off. It was still beautiful but rather startling.

Then He leaned over again and asked, "Would you like to see it in yellow?" Of course I said yes. And in an instant all of the red turned to shades of yellow. Wow! Talk about bright. Then He leaned over and asked again, this time if I'd like to see it in green. I agreed and the yellow instantly changed to shades of green. The green was lovely also, but nothing was as peaceful as the lavender. With this thought, the garden instantly switched back to lavender. I laughed out loud. Even though my favorite color was red, He knew that a color I rarely ever notice would be the one that would give me the most peace and pleasure in this setting. So the lesson I learned that day was *God knows best.*

Seated With My Creator

One time, while walking through another garden, I came upon the Father standing beside His throne. Now I had seen His throne before, but for some reason I hadn't paid much attention to it. Now I could see that the throne was so beautiful. It wasn't golden, but was made out of the substance of Heaven. It looked like formed light. Then He called me forward, put His hand on the seat, and said, "Sit down."

I looked up at Him and said, "Oh no, I can't sit there, that's Your throne."

He smiled and again told me to sit down. I was standing at the front of the throne, so I put my hand upon it. My hand went through the seat like it was a fog...nothing of substance. I quickly drew my hand back, looked up at the Father, and said, "I can't sit there, I'll fall through!" Again He just smiled and told me to sit down.

Carefully, I put my little knee up on the seat, and then gingerly climbed up, thinking that I would fall through the seat at any time. I sat back and my legs stuck straight out because the throne was so large. I set my hand on my leg and my hand "fell" through my leg, and right on through the chair. So I quickly drew my hand up to my chest. I didn't understand all of the dynamics of these heavenly visions. At this point I thought that I must be spirit, and therefore, I could be "substance," but also "non-substance." After Jesus ascended and came back, He was a spirit. He walked through a wall, and yet the disciples could also touch and feel Him. Alas, another mystery.

The Picture in the Wall

Then the Father pointed to what looked like a black obsidian wall that was standing in front of us. This wall was not smooth, however. It had facets like a diamond ring, and there were colors in each facet. All of a sudden I heard a click. As I watched, two facets in the upper right hand corner of the wall turned and became one facet. Then I heard more clicking and began to see other facets in the wall join with each other.

I looked to the Father thinking He might explain it to me. Oh, you should have seen the joy on His face. He was so excited to watch all of the little facets joining together. He looked down at me and told me to watch. I turned back and watched for a few minutes, but I was more fascinated by His expression of joy. So I scooted back in the seat of the throne so I could be a little back from Him and could watch Him again. He turned to me again and gave me a look that said, "Please watch this." I decided that I had better do what He asked. As I watched, I found that the bits of color in each facet were actually coming together to form a picture.

When all of the facets in the wall had finished clicking, the wall made one big picture of a beautiful garden. Oh my! The trees, plants, pond, and stream were breathtakingly beautiful. I realized then that He had made this "picture" just for me. He created this just for my pleasure. And the joy I had seen in His expression was because He had created something for one of

His children and was excited that He could be there with me when I discovered what He had done.

As I was enjoying the scene of the picture, He asked if I wanted to go in. Go in? Of course I said yes. He took my hand and we stepped down off the throne and walked right up to the picture. We didn't stop but walked right on into the garden. What I thought was a flat picture was actually a real garden. He so loves gardens. The trees and plants in this garden were very unusual. The colors were like none I have ever seen on earth. Such beauty is hard to comprehend.

Then we walked over near the pond and sat down. I sat on His lap and laid my head on His chest. I think it was probably similar to John laying his head on Jesus. I was resting there, just enjoying being with Him, when I heard something. I sat up so I could look up at Him, but He was just looking off into the distance. I laid my head back down and again I heard something. I sat up straight and looked at Him again. I did this a few more times until I realized that what I was hearing was Him talking. I sat up and said, "You're talking!"

He smiled and said "Yes, I am always talking. The issue is, are you listening?"

CHAPTER 23

THE FOUNTAIN

I thought about the miniature village where the Holy Spirit was tied up and I thought about how I tried to direct the growth of the box with the fuzz ball. I realized that so often we have a tendency to try to control what God is doing. God gave me another lesson on this subject one day after I read the following Scripture:

For My people have committed two evils:

They have forsaken Me,

The fountain of living waters,

To hew for themselves cisterns,

Broken cisterns

That can hold no water (Jeremiah 2:13).

Immediately after I read this verse, the Lord took me into a vision. I saw a fountain with water flowing out of it. There were lots of people around the fountain drinking, splashing, and having a good time. I noticed that the flow of the water was strong at times and ebbed at other times. At its strongest flow, it actually sprayed over the edges of the bowl, and when it ebbed, there was barely a trickle running down the fountain, but it still supplied the bowl. The people noticed this change in flow too. Someone said, "Let's go build a cistern to hold the water. You never know, the fountain may stop someday and then we would be out of water. Plus, it's being wasted when it flows over the bowl."

So a bunch of people went some distance from the fountain and built a cistern. The people got buckets and started taking the water from the fountain to the cistern. When the cistern was filled, they went about with their lives and took their water from the cistern instead of the fountain.

However, there was a problem. This cistern had a leak. It was a slow leak, so the people didn't realize that the water level was dropping. When new people came around who hadn't seen the full cistern, they just thought it was at the level it had always been. Over a long period of time, the water was reduced to mere puddles in the bottom of the cistern. People had to lie on the ground and reach down into the cistern in order to get some water. By this time the water had grown stagnant, but the people didn't even notice that the water tasted foul. They were dull, never thinking about where they had received the water in the beginning.

Then someone finally remembered the fountain and got everyone excited. They traveled back to the fountain, which wasn't far. The water was still flowing and they raced to it, drinking, splashing, and having a good time. They were revived. But eventually the cycle started all over again. Someone said, "Let's go build a cistern to hold the water...."

This Scripture and vision give us a picture of revival history. The water represents the move of the Holy Spirit. There are those who say the same things about the move of God that people said about the fountain. When the water overflowed onto the ground, people said that it was being wasted. Because they couldn't see the effect the overflowing water was having, they assumed it was unnecessary or perhaps dangerous. No doubt it was muddy around the fountain. Messy. Perhaps the excessive water caused weeds to grow around the fountain.

But it is God who causes the fountain to flow at the pressure He desires. We should not presume to judge the effects of the move of God prematurely. Perhaps the water that is soaking into the ground is forming a reservoir that will provide a well for someone in the future. Maybe someone will come along and use the mud to give sight to a blind man. As for the weeds—what if what we assume is just a weed is really a beautiful flowering plant instead? I know that I've seen plants that I thought were weeds and they turned into beautiful flowers. I've also seen plants that I thought were really pretty and it turned out they were weeds that overtook the flowers. God knows and God lets His fountain flow how He wants it to flow. By the way, the fountain isn't a circular fountain. The water is always fresh. It's not recycled. Neither is it a pool. The water is always flowing. If water sits, it loses its oxygen...the breath of God. It has to be allowed to flow to stay fresh.

Why?

Why did the people build a cistern? Fear! "What if the water stops?" they asked. Fear brings distrust of the Trustworthy One. Notice that God said through Jeremiah, *"They have forsaken Me, the fountain of living waters."* Likewise, Psalm 68:26 says, *"Bless God in the congregations, even the Lord, You who are of the fountain of Israel."* God is the fountain and the fountain is ours forever. Is it possible for God to ever dry up? Psalm 37:3 says, *"Trust in the Lord and do good; dwell in the land and cultivate faithfulness."* Don't forsake Him because you don't understand everything or because you think something negative may happen in the future. Have faith that God truly does know best! When the water is flowing very slowly and it looks like it may stop, it is time for our faith to step up to the plate. God said He would never leave us. His fountain will never stop and it will never dry up. The bowl will never be empty. The slow seasons are opportunities for us to learn to appreciate the overflowing times more. Certainly He wants us to learn to trust Him whether things are flowing fast or slow.

The cistern is a picture of how we try to control and contain what God is doing. When we open the door to fear, we allow a spirit of control to enter. Whatever you control becomes stagnant. It may happen over a long or short period of time, but it will happen every time. When we don't trust God, we do things our way. We try to control what He's given us. The problem with trying to control things is that it extinguishes the move of the Holy Spirit. This grieves Him because it communicates that we do not trust Him and merely want the benefits of His presence instead of His presence itself. Hopefully that is something none of us wants to be known for. How could we desire anything more than His presence?

It's important to note that the book of Jeremiah says that forsaking the fountain and building cisterns are two evils. These aren't just little mistakes or sins; they are actually described as "evils." One of the meanings of *evil* in Hebrew is "destroy." Fear and control destroy the works of God.

CHAPTER 24

THE PATH TO DESTINY

The Golden Brick Path

One day Jesus came and took me up to a place where a long path made of what appeared to be golden bricks stretched before us. He pointed down the path and said, "This is your path to walk on." Then He reached out His hand to me and said, "Let's go for a walk." I put my little hand in His and off we went.

After we had walked down this path for some time, I noticed something odd. Every so often I saw some strange little bars growing in groups along the edges of the path. The bars were golden and about an inch in diameter. At first the bars were few and infrequent, but then they started multiplying. Each bar grew slowly and at different levels.

Though the presence of these bars became increasingly obvious, Jesus never said anything about them. After passing by several groups of bars, I pulled my hand out of Jesus' hand and walked over to a group of bars. I just couldn't figure out what they were. As I looked at the bars, they began to grow and multiply more quickly. I walked around them as they grew, trying to figure out what they were. Jesus called to me and said, "Come." I went back to Jesus, put my hand in His hand and we started to walk again.

We had walked just a little way when I began to wonder how big those bars had grown. I started to turn around to look at them when Jesus said, "Don't look back." He wasn't mean or mad about it, but He was very firm. I looked up at Him and He bent down until we were face to face. He told me that those bars on my path were obstacles, explaining that the more I looked at them the faster they would grow, eventually blocking my path. He told me, however, that even if the obstacles grew and completely blocked my path, I could still climb over them. It wouldn't be easy once the bars blocked the path because they were of different heights. Getting a toehold would be hard, but it could be done. He reminded me that the Holy Spirit is a Helper who helps anyone who asks.

He then swept His arm toward the left of my path and I saw many, many other paths. Jesus said, "These are other people's paths. You must never walk on someone else's path." He told me that if I walked on someone else's path, two things could happen. First, that person might think I was doing the work on his or her path, so either he would sit back and not do the work he needed to do, or secondly, he would become angry with me for trespassing on his path. By walking where

I wasn't intended to walk I had the potential to either keep someone from his destiny or cause dissension in the Body of Christ. Jesus went on to tell me that I didn't have the gifting, talents, or anointing to accomplish the work on anyone else's path. It was important that I only walk on my path, ignoring all obstacles, pressing onward with my eyes toward the goal and my hand in His.

What a good lesson this was! I started thinking about what the obstacles might be. I realized that any sin could be an obstacle, and obstacles had the potential to kill my destiny. One obstacle that I see very frequently as I minister to people is offense. People take offense whenever someone does or says something that causes them anger, resentment, hurt, displeasure, or humiliation. As we each walk our paths, the most important thing to do is forgive anyone who does something to us to cause those feelings. If we don't, the obstacle of offense grows. And the more we watch the offense, the bigger the obstacle grows.

The Tale of Offense

Let me tell you a story about offense. "Fred" was 29 years old when the obstacle of offense grew up on his path. At the time, Fred was on fire for God. He was in all of the musicals at church, led a home group, and had his children in the Christian school. His passion and devotion were completely genuine. But then Fred got offended. Within a year of the unforgiven offense, Fred had left the church, and within two years he had left his wife and family. He lived a wild life for a few years. Every once in a while we saw him back at church.

He was trying to get over the offense but never seemed able to do so.

He finally remarried and settled down from his wild lifestyle but "things" took over. He loved his friends and family, but he never got on with the path to his destiny. Fred died suddenly at age 49. It was tragic. As I sat at his memorial service and listened to all of his friends talk about what a good guy he was, I was so thankful for God's grace. I had such a peace that Fred was with the Lord, partaking in the pleasure of God's presence. Did he fulfill the destiny of his path? No, but he never denied Jesus. He was still a believer.

As the service continued I had a vision of Fred in Heaven with Jesus. They were both so happy, hugging each other. And very excitedly, Jesus said, "Would you like to see all the plans I had for you?" They turned and watched the plans unfold. On Fred's path I could see numerous salvations, healings, people being set free, etc. But also on the path were the obstacles that had grown so large they completely covered the path. These were the areas that Fred was never able to overcome. Then Fred started sobbing. Jesus immediately turned to him and wiped the tears from his eyes and He said, "It's OK, Fred. You are here with Me now." I could see that Jesus was not angry or judgmental with Fred. He was just excited for Fred to see all that He had planned for him.

As soon as I saw Fred and Jesus walking away together, this Scripture came to mind, *"And He will wipe away every tear from their eyes..."* (Rev. 21:4). In the past I had wondered, *Why would we be crying in Heaven?* That verse made no sense to me. But in that moment I wondered, *What if, when we are with the Lord, He turns around and shows us our path? What if He shows us all the wonderful things that He had planned for us?* If so, we might also see all of the times that obstacles had kept us from His wonderful plans for us. Maybe the obstacles hadn't completely stopped us, but they had slowed our progress down. We might be able to see all of the obstacles and how big they had become because we insisted on dwelling on them. If that happened, I think we would be crying. Thankfully, Jesus will wipe away our tears and say, "But I paid for that. Enter into eternity in God's presence."

I cried as I thought of Fred and his untraveled path. I'm sure many people around me thought that I was crying for Fred, and they would have been right. He was a bright star who had been dulled by an obstacle of offense. But I was also crying for myself. I cried out to Jesus, "Please, please don't ever let me dwell on the obstacles. I want to accomplish everything You have for me on my path. Remind me, Jesus, of my path. Remind me not to look at obstacles. I don't ever want offense to hinder my walk. Holy Spirit, my Helper, help me."

Then there was Danny, who was 15 years old when he became offended. Actually, both men were offended by the same thing at the same time. Danny also left the church, and for the next 20 years he ran from God. He always said he believed, but his life didn't show it. Drugs and drinking consumed him. After 20 years he looked like death, and he knew he had to do something.

One day he asked his mother what made her happy. She shared with him that loving and serving Jesus made her happy, and she then proceeded to prophesy destiny into his life. He cried, but there was no outward change. Then, a few months later, he came to church with her one Sunday and went forward at the altar call. He started to meet with a couple of the pastors at the church. One of them, Banning Liebscher, was in charge of part of the second year program of Bethel School of Supernatural Ministry (BSSM). This pastor asked Danny to come up to class so they could talk in the back during class. The day he went, the students were learning about prophecy and were practicing giving prophetic words. One of the students said he had heard a name. It just so happened that it was Danny's last name. They called Danny up to the front of the class and the students began to prophesy words about his path and his destiny.

The next day he told his mother that he wanted to go to BSSM. He completed two years of the school. Danny saw his path and is walking on it. He's excited. He was able, with the Holy Spirit's help, to crawl over the obstacle of offense that had blocked his path for so many years. I am excited along with him because Danny is my son.

So that's "The Tale of Offense." One never got over the obstacle and one did. Remember what Jesus told me? Well, it really goes for all of us. "Walk only on your path. Keep your eyes forward toward the goal. Do not pay any attention to the obstacles. Keep your hand in His."

Here is an encouraging "warning." One of the big obstacles in my life was rejection. To this day, twelve years after the start of this journey, because of incidents in my life, I can still feel the sting of rejection. I can choose to look at that obstacle or I can go to Jesus and have it healed. I choose to follow Paul's admonition and take my thoughts captive (see 2 Cor. 10:5). Do people do things to all of us that aren't very nice? Yes. Whether it's on purpose or something they didn't even know they did, forgiveness is the key and then go on with your life. He never rejects us He only loves us with loving-kindness. His Love is sufficient for all my needs.

Looking at obstacles is a choice. Let your mind dwell on the good (see Phil. 4:8).

Higher

One day Jesus told me to come with Him. As we started walking, I saw a very large mountain range up ahead. After we climbed up to the very top, Jesus began walking along a ridge. I was feeling extremely tired and asked if we could just rest a few minutes before we continued our journey. He said we could rest. Then He sat down with his legs crossed Indian style, picked me up, and sat me on His lap.

I looked out over to the places I had been. Way off in the distance I could see the chasm and the bridge where I had begun this journey. I could see the maize place, the garden, the holy place with the objects, the jungle, and the orchard. Through it all ran the river of God's glory. I followed the river with my eyes. It appeared to end where the mountains began, only I knew it didn't end there but continued to flow beneath the mountains.

I was sad to be leaving these places behind. I felt so comfortable here, but as I looked around I didn't see my Father or my Holy Spirit anywhere. I didn't want to stay where I could not be with Them. I knew They were up ahead waiting for me, and my Jesus would take me to Them.

CHAPTER 25

TAKING OTHERS TO HEAVEN

At Bethel School of Supernatural Ministry (BSSM) near the start of each new school term, the leadership has me come to "do my Heaven thing." I do this at the beginning of the term because that's when heart and relationship issues between the students and the Father are being dealt with.

The most important thing I have found about leading people to the gate of Heaven is that it's all about relationship with the Father, Son, and Holy Spirit. My natural father did not love me—didn't know how to love me—and this so affected the way I saw God the Father. It is difficult to feel that God loves you when you haven't actually experienced being loved by your own father. Oh, I knew the Bible said that God loved me, but I had never actually experienced this love before the Father so profoundly showed me how much He loved me.

I so love leading people to the place where they experience God in a new, loving, and wonderful way. When I start telling people about what happened to me I get caught up in the wonder of it all over again—the wonder of how God so loves us and wants to manifest Himself to us. I feel the joy of a little girl with her daddy. As I look around the room, it seems as though the students are caught up in the wonder as well.

I share with them how much it looks like imagination, but it comes from one's spirit, and it is with the leading of the Holy Spirit. I tell the students to relax and be peaceful, because they can't enter into an encounter when they are striving. By this time, their excitement is palpable in the air, sort of like children going on their first ride at Disneyland.

The Process

Here is how I lead others past their obstacles and into the Kingdom, where they can begin to see with the eyes of their spirit, the only One who is pure love—Jesus. Come along with us. He is here for you too.

First, I tell them to close their eyes and not to open them until I give them permission. Then I tell them to picture Jesus out in front of them. He doesn't have to be real clear because when I first saw Him it was shadowy. I wait and then ask them to raise their hands if they have a picture of Him. I know that there will always be some who aren't seeing anything, but I know I can't wait for everyone, so if the majority can picture Him, I tell the rest to soak in His presence.

Next I tell the students to walk up to Jesus and then wait. I ask again how many are standing right in front of Him. By this time His presence is growing very strong because we have entered into a heavenly atmosphere where people are anxious for an encounter with a loving God. Then I tell them that He is going to do something.

How do I know? Because this is what He told me to do. I don't understand all the whys and wherefores. I'm just a little girl trying to share the love of my Abba/Daddy. This is where it starts to get very interesting.

I have them raise their hands if Jesus has done something. Then I go around to them with a microphone and ask them what He did. Their eyes are still closed because I don't want them to be distracted. Oh the things I hear. "He hugged me." "He kissed me." "He's dancing with me." "He put His hand on my head." It's that touch. Jesus loves to touch us. Isn't that the way love is here in our world? When we love someone we want to be near them, we want to touch them. Do you really think it's any different with Him?

Then I tell them that He wants to say something to them. I wait for a while. Then I go to the people who have raised their hands in affirmation that Jesus has spoken to them and have them share. "I love you." I'm proud of you." "I have so many wonderful things to show you." "I have a plan for your life."

Father has told me that He has created a garden for everyone. Not a community garden (although He may have one of those too) but a special garden for everyone. So I tell the students that and have them ask Jesus to take them there.

Sometimes Jesus takes them other places, but most of the time they go to their gardens.

I give them some time to spend there to see what Jesus will do. Again the stories afterward are marvelous. By this time some are crying softly as Jesus touches their hearts, some are smiling broadly, and others are not moving a muscle as if they are afraid it will all go away. The presence of God is so strong in the place. I love His presence and love how He heals our hearts.

I always find a time afterward to meet with the ones who don't see anything. I spend time with them in a group answering questions, talking to them, sharing how God wants them to come be with Him even more than they want to go. There are always a few who don't see, but I seek God on that because I think everyone has the capacity to see. These students just don't yet understand how they see.

I want to be clear that not everyone who sees into the third Heaven realm is a seer or prophet. The heavenly interactions I've described above are available to all of us. But just because we have these Third Heaven experiences does not mean that we function in the office of the prophet, such as people like Bob Jones, Bobby Conner, Paul Keith Davis, or Rick Joyner. The purpose of these heavenly experiences is to connect you to the loving-kindness of our wonderful Father, Son, and Holy Spirit.

Recently I spoke at the school of ministry at Bethel-Atlanta, which is one of our church plants. The pastors of Bethel-Atlanta, Steve and Lindy Hale, had been in BSSM before they went back home to start a church. It was so amazing. Have you ever felt God's presence so strongly that you just wanted to sit down and soak it all in? This presence feels like "heavy air," and it carries with it His peace, love, kindness, and so much more.

We played Kimberly and Alberto's *Live Soaking Volume 1* CD and I had them play "Show Me Your Face" over and over. When you find a worship song that moves your spirit, it is the perfect place to be able to enter into His presence. Listening to worship music prepares your heart to give worship (a kiss) to Him and to receive His kisses in return. I led the students as I described earlier, and the results were amazing. I love to look out and see big, manly men with their eyes closed and tears streaming down their cheeks. Sometimes I even see people mouth words as they are talking to Him. I love the Lord's presence and love to see others come into His presence and have their hearts touched by Him.

The Three "Heavens"

I went to a church where the pastors are good friends of mine to do a women's retreat. About a week later I received an e-mail from one of the pastors asking me what she should do in a situation she had run into. It seems that one of the women was seeing something that may not have been third Heaven experiences. There are three "heavens" or "realms." I love how Beni Johnson teaches about these realms in her book *The Happy Intercessor*:

> There are three "realms" that are mentioned in the Bible. The word realm means "source" or "on each side." The Bible specifically talks about the first

realm, the second realm and the third realm. The first realm is the realm that you can see with you eyes. It's the physical realm. *"Then I saw a new heaven and a new Earth, for the first heaven and the first earth had passed away. Also there was no more sea"* (Rev. 21:1). So here you can see that the first heaven is the earthly realm, or what you can see right now. Our bodies, our homes, and our cities exist in the earthly realm. Deuteronomy 10:14 (NKJV) says, *"Indeed heaven and the highest heavens belong to the Lord your God, also the Earth with all that is in it."* According to the New American Standard Exhaustive Concordance of the Bible, the word heaven means, "astrologers, compass, Earth, heaven, heavens, and the highest heaven those, from the beginning, God created the earth, the heavens, and the highest heavens."

The second heaven, or "mid-heaven" of Revelation 14:6, *"and I saw another angel flying in mid-heaven, having an eternal gospel to preach to those who live on the Earth and to every nation and tribe and tongue and people"* (NASB version), is the demonic and angelic realm where there is war going on between the angelic and demonic. In Daniel the second realm is the demonic angelic realm. That's the realm where there is warfare, and the negative comes out.

Then, there is the third realm. This realm is where the glory of God is. It's the beauty realm. The apostle Paul calls the third heaven "paradise." It's where we can see the great plans of heaven. *"I know a man in*

Christ who 14 years ago, whether in the body I do not know, or whether out of the body, I do not know, God knows. God knows such a one was caught up to the third heaven..." (2 Cor. 12:2). He continues in verse 4, "*...how he was caught up into paradise and heard inexpressible words....*"[1]

So you can see how experiencing the second realm or second Heaven would not be a positive experience. It is possible for some people to have visions of that place, similarly to experiencing third Heaven visions. Someone I knew who had taken LSD said about their experience, "You see things God never meant you to see." How prophetic for a pre-Christian to have such insight and use such words. When you are seeking God with all of your heart, you don't have to be afraid of having second Heaven visions. If you spend time in the Word of God, you will know if what you are experiencing lines up with what He has already said or if it is a contradiction. Another safeguard to being deceived by our enemy is to be rightly connected to the Body of Christ and in right relationship with others.

Tools

I remember when I first started learning about prophecy during the Charismatic Renewal. At that time there was quite a bit of controversy and numerous "words" that definitely were not of God, not to mention the excesses and misuses of speaking in tongues. The gifts of the Spirit are tools that God gives us to help us in establishing His Kingdom. Having heavenly experiences is a tool God will use to show us who

He really is and how He works and even gives us strategies for establishing His Kingdom: "*Your kingdom come, Your will be done*" (Matt. 6:10). Tools are meant to be used in specific ways. You don't use a hammer to cut a piece of wood in two. Obviously, if you want to cut wood you would choose a saw for your tool. When you're teaching someone, you work with them to show them how to use the correct tool in the proper way. You certainly don't throw the hammer away because it doesn't cut wood.

In regard to spending time with the Lord, it is important to understand that quantity will not always get you quality. Now I am not saying that you shouldn't spend a significant amount of time with Him. What I am saying is that even a little bit of time is precious to Him. Sometimes we are so busy that we let time pass by, thinking that if we can't spend a lot of time, it doesn't count.

Let me tell you a story about my boys, Jon and Danny, and show you how breaking things into smaller increments helps you achieve what you thought was going to be a very huge and difficult task. When my boys were 10 and 12 years of age we lived in a home that was heated by a wood-burning stove. One year at the beginning of summer we had three cords of wood delivered into a huge pile in our yard. That is a tremendous amount of logs because one cord of wood is approximately 4 feet wide by 4 feet high by 8 feet long.

Now their dad told them they had to take all of this wood and stack it in the woodshed. Well, you can imagine the complaining I heard from my sons! They said they wouldn't be able to play all summer because they would be working. On and on they lamented. So I walked out into the yard with them and told them not to worry. I wanted each of them to just put five pieces of wood into the shed each morning. Their eyes got wide as they realized this would be much easier than they had thought. Suddenly, the task didn't seem nearly so difficult.

The first morning I watched them through the kitchen window as they each picked up five logs and stacked them. When they came out of the shed they said they could do more than that. So they each made a few more trips to the woodshed. Later that day, they made a few more trips. This went on for a week. By the end of the week, what they thought would take all summer was finished. Simply breaking the job down into smaller pieces did what had seemed impossible at the beginning.

When we look at what appears to be a huge task we can get overwhelmed. But when we break it down into smaller, more manageable pieces we keep ourselves from getting too discouraged to even try. Spending time with the Lord in our busy world can seem overwhelming. For the mother of little children who feels like she never has time to herself, the exhausted working mother trying to meet the obligations of work and family, and the man who has to work several jobs to make ends meet, I want to say there is time for you to spend with the most wonderful God ever.

Start by spending just a few minutes with Him. Close your eyes, turn your heart's attention to Him, and tell Him hello! Practice. You'll find your time with Him lengthening. In His presence is such peace, joy, love, and acceptance. He does not say that because you don't give Him an hour, He's unhappy with you. Would an hour be good? Yes, but don't turn it into a heavy law that you have to keep. Start with five "logs" per day.

Endnote

1. Beni Johnson, *The Happy Intercessor*, (Destiny Image Publishers, Inc, 2009), 92-93.

CHAPTER 26

BRINGING KRYSTAL TO HEAVEN

In December of 1998 a man who had a prophetic gifting came to speak at Bethel, and he happened to attend one of our board meetings. Pastor Bill Johnson had asked him to speak to the board and he prophesied over each board member. I was taking the minutes for the meeting. Toward the end he called me up and prophesied the following:

> The Spirit of the Lord says, I have reserved for you a catching up. And the Lord says you would be the last to think that you could have a third Heaven experience. But you have asked for things, said things, and the Lord says why shouldn't I take you up on it? Why shouldn't I allow you, why shouldn't I let you?

Well, I had been praying for 30 years to have a third Heaven experience and this man was prophesying that God was going to answer my prayer. I was overwhelmed. The next night I was with the Father, just like I had been so many times before. He asked me if I wanted to go to the third Heaven. I excitedly said yes and He took my hand and we took off.

After just a little bit, we stopped at a beautiful garden that looked quite familiar. I realized that this was the first garden I had seen in my visions, and I was a bit confused. So I turned to the Father and said, "But I've been here before."

He said, "Yes, I know." Then He started laughing. It was then that I realized that somehow I wasn't just having little visions, but I had actually been entering the realm of the third Heaven.

Krystal

At some point someone gave me a note and asked me to take it to Jesus the next time I went to Heaven. I read the note and it said, "Dear Father, I need some money. Your loving son." I laughed about it and put it away, not thinking about it again. However, the next time I went to Heaven, the Father said, "Give Me the note." I thought, *What note?* I looked down and there in my hand was the note. So I gave it to Him and He read it. Then He threw His head back and laughed and said, "I love him so much. He makes Me laugh."

That was amazing in itself, but the next week someone gave that man $1,000. Well, the story got around and one day my good friend Krystal came to me with a note. Krystal had lost her only two children in a tragic car accident several years earlier. Her note said, "Dear Father, I want to see my boys." I stuck the note in my purse and didn't read it until later that night. I was thinking it was probably just another funny note, but after I read the note I was sobered and saddened.

That night when I was with Jesus again, I asked Him what I should say to Krystal. He just smiled and out of the corner of my eye I saw movement. I looked and saw her two boys walking up to me. This frightened me and I began to back up, saying, "This can't happen. I'm so sorry, I'm doing something wrong." I was thinking about Deuteronomy 18:11-12 which forbids "spiritists" to call up the dead. I knew I hadn't called them, but I was certainly seeing them. Then Jesus caught my arm and very gently pulled me up to Him. The boys started telling me about Heaven and how wonderful it was and how much fun they were having. Then one of them took my hand and put a gold locket in it. I glanced at it and saw that it was solid gold with etching on the outside edge. He closed my hand over it and said, "Give this to my mother. It's hers." Then the vision was over.

I decided I would not tell Krystal what had happened because she would be so hurt that I saw her boys without her being able to experience it. I had no idea what the locket was about, and I had no plans to mention it. Well, the next day I was in my office and Krystal walked by. As soon as I saw her, the Lord said, "I want you to tell her." I immediately said, "No way." Didn't He realize how much this would hurt her? (A real "duh!" moment for me.) The Lord asked me again, and after struggling for a bit I went in and told her about my encounter with her boys. As you can imagine it was a very tearful time for both of us. Krystal asked me about the locket but gave me no further information about it.

"Bring Her"

That afternoon the Lord said, "I want you to bring her to Me." *What?* I thought, *how can I bring her to You? I don't know how to do that.* This time He didn't repeat the command because He knew I had heard. So I went back to Krystal's office and told her what I had heard.

As we were sitting in an empty office, I prayed, "OK God, how do we do this?" I took her hand and immediately started seeing something. I asked her if she saw anything, but she said she couldn't. Krystal told me she wasn't a visual person and didn't have dreams or visions—or even imagine things. OK, so now what? I finally told her that I would tell her what I was seeing. I could see us both as little girls and I described what we were wearing and what we looked like. Within this heavenly realm there was a garden with beautiful flowers and a weeping willow tree. In the middle was a wrought iron table and chairs with a tea set in the middle of the table. Jesus took her over to the table and they had a tea party.

The next morning Krystal brought in her writing pad, a hard-topped surface with a soft cushion underneath that you can set on your lap to write on. Every morning she would go up in her loft, put her writing pad on her lap, and do her daily devotional with the Lord. On the hard top was a picture of a garden with beautiful flowers and a weeping willow tree with a wrought iron table and chairs with a tea set. It was exactly what I saw when I took her to Heaven. I believe that God was really showing Krystal how He meets her every morning in this garden of her quiet time.

About two weeks later she came in to the office to show me something. In her hand was a gold locket with etching around the outside. Her son had given it to her for Christmas just seven days before he died. She had lost the locket several months earlier, and she and her husband had turned the house upside down looking for it. After I had shared that her son had given me the locket, she was cleaning out her car and noticed a lump on the driver's side floor mat. When she pulled the carpet up there was the locket! She said as soon as I told her about the locket she knew that she would find it again. God is so good!

The term that has just sort of developed for having this experience of a heavenly vision is "going to Heaven." Since that time with Krystal I've been asked many times to lead people into these sorts of visits with God. It may not be the most accurate description, but around here many of us call this process of leading another "taking someone to Heaven."

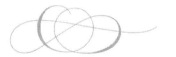

CHAPTER 27

TESTIMONIES

What follows is a sampling of the many positive testimonies I've received from sharing my journey and encouraging others in these sorts of experiences. (The following testimonies were given to me in written form with permission to be used in this book.)

Ian Kilpatrick started a website called BeenUp2 (www. beenup2.com). It's a wonderful way to stay connected through pictures and little comments. Ian Kilpatrick is a Christian and I knew his dad, a Christian musician, years ago. Ian messaged me on BeenUp2 and asked me about going to Heaven. I sent him a DVD that had been filmed when I was teaching at the BSSM. After his encounter he wrote:

> It has helped me rediscover how simple God is in how He visits us. It's not work. This was what I needed.

I've had breakthrough in it and am discovering new things about Him and how to visit regularly.

Yeah, God. That's what I want...to connect. It isn't work, it is what everyone needs, and I love doing it.

One of my favorite stories comes from a woman in Washington, who came weeping to me after her experience to tell me what had happened. She told me that she had followed along as I taught, prayed, and led in a "Heaven" experience, although she did not expect anything to happen. However, she had the most wonderful time. When she was with Jesus, all of her clothing turned to the whitest of whites. She spent time with Him in a beautiful dress and her hair was so beautiful. They danced together and then sat and talked. It seems pretty simple, but to her it was monumental. Because of her past, she never thought she was clean. She knew the Bible said she was, but she never saw herself as clean. Jesus made it very evident to her that she was washed clean as snow. After this she had a whole new relationship with her God.

Latane's Story

Another healing of the heart took place in a meeting in Georgia during a prayer experience where each person is not talking or asking God anything, just quietly soaking and enjoying His presence. Here's the story:

> Some of us can only imagine what we will do when we see Jesus face to face...well I know because I went to the third Heaven. I fell at Jesus' feet and He said, "Look at Me, my beloved." I felt unworthy and started

to kiss His hand that He had extended to me...and instead He cupped my cheeks and I felt the most incredible love—that is indescribable.

The next day I had to get back to the third Heaven. During soaking I felt the warm touch of Jesus on my cheek again. I knew I was in Heaven again. This time I took hold of His hand and He was to take me to my own personal garden. I was so excited with anticipation of what it would be like...my own garden in Heaven. Wow, it had to have the most extravagant colors imaginable.

So I walked with Jesus and we came to an opening. There it was. Only it wasn't as I had imagined. It was a dirt patch—no flowers, no waterfall. I was so confused. I turned and asked Jesus, "Is this my garden??? Why Lord? Why a garden of dirt? Surely you love me more than this."

Jesus responded, "Of course I love you" and He smiled.

Then I started to recognize where I was. It was a place from my childhood. My paternal grandmother's yard where we children ran and played. There was dirt, because grass could not grow under our constant play. I asked Jesus, "Why here? Surely this isn't my garden." Jesus said, "I brought you here because this is the last place you truly felt that your earthly daddy loved you, and I want you to know that he loves you just as much today. Even though you don't feel that he loves you, he loves you with all the love he is capable of giving." This hit my heart so deeply and this truth healed my deep wounds.

Even though that garden was not the one I had imagined I would go to, it was the most incredible garden because there was healing in that garden. There was much reconciliation and a renewed love relationship with my Daddy Father during my visit to Heaven. That healing led to forgiveness and that forgiveness led to an open heaven that invaded my daddy's heart and he accepted Jesus three days before he died. "Yeah God."

Isn't that wonderful? A visit with God brought about a reconciliation. It wasn't spoken harshly or cruelly but in gentleness. After all, God is Love and love is one of the fruits of the Spirit. Do we think that He has told us to be gentle and He is not? Look what she put on Facebook:

TGIF—Thank God I'm Forgiven! I may mess up...but the Lord—He loves me beyond my mess...He loves when He says He loves...not just when I'm good...how can I not PRAISE HIM WITH ALL MY BEING!!!

Gisele's Story

This testimony came from a first-year student, Gisele, who attends our BSSM.

It is amazing to be here at Bethel and hear story after story of the encounters that people have had with Him. It's a place like no other! I was excited about going to Heaven that night because my husband and I had a pretty rough experience over the weekend. So I invited him along this time. He is not a BSSM student at this time, but is in a men's group that you had spoken to last fall. He was really blessed and looking forward to this evening as well. The Lord showed me that my "love tank" was empty. This was not something I had expected to see. The music began, and I met Jesus in my garden at the table we usually meet at. As I sat and joined Him, I just began to pour my heart out to Him—one thing after another. I told Him my frustrations, hurts, and all the things that had been happening lately. He looked at me and listened with His undivided attention.

He then took my hand and said, "I want to show you something." We ran together through the garden, passing by other things that He had shown me in the past. He never let go of my hand, until we got to where He wanted to show me what He had for me. It was a field full of red flowers. At first, it looked like an endless field of red tulips—like you would see in a catalog. But as I looked closer, it was a field full of red heart flowers. He said, "This is all for you."

Then He told me that He was the One who could fill me up. I had been looking to others to fill up what only He could fill up with His love. He bent over and scooped His arms full of hearts and began throwing them at me in a playful way. I could see them going into my "love tank" and it was beginning to get filled up because I had come to "the Source." The field was endless! He just kept scooping them up and throwing them at me. He told me that they were all mine and I could come anytime to get more.

It was amazing! This is what I had been missing. He has a beautiful smile by the way! I had been feeling this "emptiness/void inside" if you will, for maybe three plus years now. I couldn't figure out what it was. He revealed it to me instantly in this time of meeting Him. He filled me up with His love, like only He could. I had been taking care of many family members with very serious illnesses and injuries for almost two years. I am a nurse and was able to do this. But I hadn't been replenishing what I had been giving out. But, in a moment in Heaven with Him, He gave me what I needed and more. He showed me the place I can go anytime to be filled up with Him. His love is endless.

Connie's Story

My father did not approve of me as a child and even more so as I grew up and began to have a different idea/relationship with God than what my dad had. It was always tense when the family got together, and I was always trying to earn his approval.

One time in prayer God assured me that when my dad got to Heaven, He would tell my dad I was really saved. That released me to pursue God with a new freedom.

I attended one of Judy's classes on soaking that opened up a new avenue for me to pursue God. Then I saw one of her DVDs on going to Heaven.

I did not have my dad in mind as I put on the music and lay on the floor before the Lord.

As I drew closer to the Lord, I saw my dad standing on the other side of Jesus. He was younger looking and laughing. I understood this was the dad he had always wanted to be: perfect, happy, and full of love for me. We did not need to exchange words but I "knew." It was all I needed to change the image of an angry distant dad to the loving dad I had always wanted.

I tell you the truth, or as Jesus said so many times, "Verily, verily," our Father wants to heal all our "daddy" issues. He is not like our earthly fathers. Even it they are really good, they are not the best, but He is.

Miles' Story

Lest you think that adults are the only ones to encounter Jesus in a remarkable way, let me tell you the story of a young boy who experienced an extraordinary healing. I was in Alabama doing some meetings and on a Saturday night I led some people to Heaven's gate. A nine-year-old boy named Miles was in one of the meetings. Afterward, I asked Miles what he had seen, and he shared with the rest of the congregation. Sometimes I am so struck by the anointing on young people. Miles was one of those children who had a wonderful anointing on him from God. The following is an account from Miles' pastor, Les Teel:

> I wanted to share with you that at the Sunday morning service our kids were doing soaking prayer in the children's ministry, and one of the 9-year-old boys who was in the conference over the weekend went to Heaven and met Jesus. In his visitation Jesus brought him a slice of pizza and said, "Here, I want you to eat this." And the boy told Jesus, "Lord, I can't eat pizza, I'm allergic to it. You know that." [Note here: This boy has more allergies than anyone I know. He is highly allergic to all dairy products, tomato sauce, citrus juices, peanuts, seafood, etc. His throat begins to close shut within a minute or two of coming into contact with these foods. His mother said she has been to the emergency room more times over his allergic reactions than she could count. She actually has to carry an Epi (epinephrine) pen with her everywhere they go. Needless to say he had a very boring diet.] Then Jesus told him, "If you will trust Me and eat this piece of pizza, I will heal you of all your allergies." So the boy took the pizza from Jesus and ate it. Then his visitation was over. After church was over

he told his mother about his visitation with Jesus at Sunday school that morning. He told her that Jesus would heal him of his allergies if he would eat the piece of pizza He gave him. And here is what really blows my mind. The mother decided to honor her son's testimony of the visitation of the Lord in her child's life. That afternoon she gave him a bowl of sherbet ice cream that had milk and citrus juices in it (two of the big no-no's). He ate it and never showed any signs of an allergic reaction.

Can you say "Big Yeah God! Big Praise to Jesus!"? I am astounded at the faith of both the mother and the child. It took great courage for her to feed her son something that had nearly killed him many times before. I'm glad she did not call me and ask me for counsel about what to do before she did this or I might have messed it up for them. Thank God! And who would have thought that Jesus would give a boy a piece of pizza in a heavenly visitation that would cure him of his food allergies?

I called Judy and asked her if she had ever had anyone get physically healed from a heavenly visitation with the Lord like what happened with this boy and she said, "No, not until now." So God is good all the time and He never ceases to amaze us with what He is going to do next. And so Judy has helped to bring us into a new dimension of healing we have never seen before. We are overwhelmed.

Jeff's Story

God healed Miles while he was having a heavenly experi-ence. Wow! Could it be that God would do that again? Jeff was a wonderful person who attended our church and was a personal friend of Bill Johnson. He had cancer and people were going over to pray for him every day. Jeff is with the Lord now. He is one of those strong soldiers who seemingly lost the battle with the enemy, but the enemy didn't win, Jeff did.

His wife, Shelly, wrote a letter to a friend with Jeff's tes-timony from this time. Recently she asked if I would like to read it. I have to say that it was hard to read through the tears streaming down my face. At the time I didn't know the effect this experience had on Jeff or his family, so this letter touched me deeply. I asked Shelly if I could include it in my book. I have lightly edited the following letter.

Dear Zac,

Bill was sending over healing teams and various leaders to come every single day, a few hours a day. I'd never heard of Judy's "gift" until she showed up, with a few others, at our house. She told us that Bill wanted her to escort Jeff to Heaven (and come back, of course...they kidded about that ☺) and ask the Father and or Jesus what was going on. Jeff was very upfront with her and the team and told them that he is, by nature and by profession, a highly critical-thinker/cynical/logical person. He told them that, though he didn't doubt Judy's experience, he knew too much about hypnotherapy to not be able to let himself "go." (Jeff used to do relaxation workshops for prison inmates...he had a heart for that population, and juvenile delinquents, and children...oh, and he really loved the old folks.) He told them that he would be willing to go along with it, but that he would tell them if he thought he was conjuring it up himself. "Fair enough," said Judy. Judy asked if I wanted to go along, and I said I'd rather observe so I could relay it back to Jeff later. Actually, a deep part of me was slightly skeptical, and I was pretty sure that Jeff was too analytical to have this "work."

Judy began by praying with Jeff and the others, and then asked Jeff to close his eyes. She did what was very reminiscent of guided imagery, that therapists and psychologists use for hypnosis and relaxation, so I thought, *Uh oh, this is not going to fly.* She spoke in a very low and slow voice, describing finding oneself in Heaven...Jeff kept interrupting, and saying, "Sorry Judy, but I think I'm forcing myself to imagine what you are saying." Judy, so serene, would say, "That's OK, Jeff, don't worry about it...just picture yourself in the heavenlies." Jeff must have stopped her at least half a dozen times...I was getting tense, because I thought this was going to be a "bust" and disappointing for all. Zac, another thing, Jeff was never the type to "act." He hated pantomime games or anything of a pretend nature...I need to preface this next part by clarifying that.

After a time, maybe 15, 20 minutes...maybe even a half hour, something changed. I could see it on Jeff's face. He looked so happy, and he looked as though he was seeing something. One of Judy's people said quietly, "Do you see the bench in the garden?" The look on Jeff's face told it all. He nodded his head to the side, as if to say "yes, and how did you know?"... kinda like "Gotcha." Judy told Jeff to go over to the bench and sit down. I could tell that Jeff was not here, but there. The feeling of the Holy Spirit was so powerful in the room, and I wanted to remember everything...goose bumps were on top of goose bumps. Jeff said, "OK, I'm sitting on the bench in the garden" and he had the most beautiful smile on his face. Judy said, "Do you see Jesus?" (I was holding my breath.) Jeff paused, as though savoring something delicious.... and he smiled, and tears began to form in his closed eyes..."Yes, He is here with me." Again. Holy Spirit was intoxicatingly overwhelming in the room. I then realized that all those people, with Jeff, could see what Jeff was seeing. They saw the bench and the garden, and Jesus. I began to wish I'd gone, too, but I really wanted to be a good reporter for Jeff when he came back.

Judy said, "Jeff, ask Jesus about your cancer." Jeff said aloud, "Jesus, tell me about this cancer." Jeff's face looked troubled, and he frowned...what he said gave me a start. "I have a giant hook in my heart. It is a hook that has been with me since I was a little boy, when I was heartbroken." (I knew what that was...Jeff's parents divorced when he was a baby, his mother married the proverbial wicked stepfather, and his mother would not intervene when he was cruel. His real father abandoned him.) Tears were running down Jeff's face, and mine. Judy said, "Ask Jesus to remove the hook." Jeff waited awhile, with various expressions crossing his face. Finally, Jeff said that Jesus had cut off the end and pulled it out. Jeff said, "I have hooks all over me." Judy said, "Ask Jesus to remove them all." Jeff's face was glowing during the moments it took to remove the hooks.

Then, someone, I can't remember if it was Judy or one of the others, said, "Does Jesus have something for you?" Again, Jeff nodded his head in acknowledgment that they knew what he knew...Jeff smiled, and said, "Why yes, Jesus is holding a present." Someone said, "Open it...it's for you!" Now, here is where I absolutely knew that Jeff could not be just going along with this...I had to look twice, as Jeff was going through the motions of untying a ribbon, and lifting a lid off what seemed to be a small square box (by the way he handled it). Jeff gave a small short surprised laugh.... We all asked, "What is it?" I was sure it would be a gem or something precious. Jeff said "A giant marshmallow. Jesus said that He is like this marshmallow.... sweet and soft and good." (Zac...Jeff has 2 favorite foods...popcorn and marshmallows.)

Jeff took his time staying with Jesus, and finally, Judy led him back. (I can't remember how she did that, and I think at the end, I was on the fringe of being there.) From that moment on, Jeff displayed an absolutely dramatic change in his person...pure love, like I'd never known him to be. The kids and I were stunned. It was instant...something about having been in Heaven with Jesus, and having his hooks cut out, did something.

Jeff is with Jesus now and can gaze upon His beauty every moment. He is also now a part of a group called the "great cloud of witnesses" cheering us on (see Heb. 12:1).

God is so good. That is such an understatement, for there are no words that can accurately portray how wonderfully good He is.

Praise the Lord!

Oh give thanks to the Lord, for He is good;

For His loving-kindness is everlasting" (Psalm 106:1).

Lizzie's Story

I received another testimony about a mom who began to take her severely autistic son to Heaven at about the age of six years. The mom had been praying for years for her son, Jordan, and the Lord had been giving her specific prayer directives. At one point the Lord told her to bring her son to Heaven. The first time Jordan described a shimmering light cloud that came and enveloped him, and the second time he saw stars and planets and a place with beautiful trees. It became a part of his nighttime routine. So just before bed she would take him to Heaven and have him describe what he saw.

One night the Lord told her to take Jordan to His throne room. In the throne room he saw the Father sitting in a rocking chair. So she told him to go run and sit in the Father's lap. He did, and as he was held in the Father arms, He began to hum a song over Jordan, telling him, "I love you, I love you." Jordan began to describe what looked like green X-rays coming toward him, which seemed to come from the Father's mouth. Green represents new life and new beginnings.

From that time on, Jordan has been making remarkable process. He's become more talkative, interacts with people, and is also able to maintain eye contact. His mom states, "If the key to healing autism is to take children to Heaven where the Father can release the song over them, then we have to get them there."

CHAPTER 28

LETTING GO AND LETTING GOD

By Beni Johnson

Many people reading this book can identify with Judy's life and say, "Yes, that's me." And some reading this may not be able to identify at all. But I'm here to tell you that we all need an encounter with the Father. I love to know that the broken will be free and will be able to sit with the Father and let Him love them and restore them through heavenly encounters. But I'm also glad that *all* may come.

You can see while reading this book that Judy does have a unique gift. Being able to help a person into an encounter with our Father is awesome.

It is our cry deep within all of us to love and have connection with God, Jesus, and the Holy Spirit.

Many years ago I had an experience where I connected to the Trinity. I've never been the same since. What I learned is that God desires for us to have heavenly encounters with Him. And, it's not a once-in-a-lifetime event. There is a saying that I used to hear, "That person is so heavenly minded, she is no earthly good." I want to tell you that is not true. The saying should really be, "They are so heavenly minded they are so earthly good." I know that's bad grammar, but you get my point.

God has so much to teach us and have us learn, and one of the ways He does this is through heavenly encounters with Him.

Judy and I were doing a women's conference in Georgia one time, and it was Judy's turn to teach in one of the sessions. She had told me she was going to share about her life and then lead everyone in having a heavenly encounter. I was so excited. I had previously experienced my own encounter but had not ever been in on hearing Judy lead people. I decided that I was not going to just sit and observe but was going to jump right in and get all that I could get. At the end of her sharing, she asked everyone who could to lie on the floor and get comfortable. Then she had us close our eyes and picture Jesus coming toward us. I immediately saw Jesus (my sanctified imagination is really alive and active). Judy then told us to see if He was saying anything to us. He told me that He loved me, and after that I don't remember what Judy said because I was caught up into Heaven.

Paul said:

> *I know a man in Christ who fourteen years ago— whether in the body I do not know, or whether out of the body I do not know, God knows—such a one was caught up to the third heaven* (2 Corinthians 12:2 NKJV).

I looked down at my clothes and I was wearing a beautiful, full-length, white cotton dress. I looked up at Jesus and He picked me up, turned around, and started walking toward a cottage. Before we got to the cottage, He put me down. I immediately knew that this was my cottage. The feeling that I was having during this time was joy. There was so much happiness. I was also feeling that this was the end of all time. All the generations were in Heaven. Eternity had started. As I was staring at this beautiful little English cottage with an English garden to my left and a grassy area to the right, I heard children coming around from the back of the cottage on the grassy lawn. The first child I saw was our oldest grandchild, Kennedy. When she saw me, she screamed to the other grandchildren, "Grandma is here now. We can play," and off she ran with the others.

All the time this was going on, I was crying. Really, that is too mild of a word. I was bawling my eyes out. Not out of sadness but out of sheer joy and happiness. I am a feeler, so feeling things is really important to me and I connect with that. Isn't it awesome that Father meets you right where it fits for you?

Anyway, I then turned to my right and looked in back of me and saw my fraternal grandmother, and she had many children with her. My dad's mom had been a Christian as long as I had known her. She had taught Sunday school for many years. She was an amazing woman. The day that my grandma retired from teaching Sunday school, she was up on the platform at church, and the leaders were honoring her for all the years she had helped out. As she was standing there on the stage being honored by the leaders and her church family, she collapsed from a stroke. Five days after that, she went to be with Jesus.

When I saw her in Heaven with all those children, it thrilled me. I realized that what she was doing for God here on earth is what she was doing in Heaven. She loved the children, and she was now loving them in Heaven too.

Then I looked again to my left side and saw my maternal grandmother. My mother's mom had been a pastor's wife for many years. But in those days she did not receive the honor that is given now to pastors and their wives. She became very bitter toward the church and my grandfather. She divorced my grandfather and lived for years in her bitterness, which eventually affected her physical body. But there were good times with Granny, and one thing I remember about her was her laugh. She was a big woman, and when she got tickled about something, she would throw her head back and open her month and laugh so loud you could see her tonsils. It made me so happy to see her happy. In this encounter, when I saw her she threw her head back and opened her month and let out a laugh that made me smile. God had erased all the hurts and she was Granny again.

I then turned my attention back to the cottage, and as I did, Bill's dad walked past me and stopped and looked at me. He said, "You are good for Bill." That's all he said and it was enough.

During the entire encounter I couldn't quite put my head around the feeling I was having. It felt familiar to me, but I couldn't figure it out. I just lay there on the floor resting in it, and then it hit me: this is peace. But what was different about this peace is that it was perfect peace. Perfect peace. Never had I felt so much peace before and so much perfection in it. It completely undid me. I didn't want to leave this feeling. There was no noise in my head. You know the kind I'm talking about—the kind that distracts you and makes you think too much. The war in my head was gone! I was lying in perfect peace. I did not want to leave. I knew that if I left this place, that peace would go away.

Then I heard Judy say, "OK, we will stop now." Inside of me, I was screaming, "No, no, no, I don't want to leave this place!" Of course we know that we do have to come back and live our lives. But isn't it wonderful that we are impacted by those times with the Trinity and we walk differently and talk differently from that point on? While I was coming to, I remembered something my husband had recently taught. He had said that when God invites you into His vineyard and gives you a gift, it is always yours. You can have it whenever you want. That day I took the gift of peace, and I know that peace is my portion all the time. My head still gets in the way, but I'm working on that.

I have had the privilege to teach on heavenly encounters and have had people share their experiences afterward. I taught on this at a workshop in one of the youth conferences that we were having at the church. When I was done teaching, I told the participants that we were going to soak in God's presence and that many of them in the room would have heavenly experiences. When we were finished, I asked them if any would like to share what happened to them. One youth raised his hand and told us that when he was three, his parents died and that when he was soaking, he was taken up into Heaven and he saw his mom and dad. Another story came from a youth pastor in the room. He was taken to the beginning of time when God was creating the world. In the sound of God speaking, he saw those things He spoke come into being. He said it was so amazing to see all the colors and things being created.

Many times we will see people healed in their encounters with God. One woman told us that God loved on her and brought some deliverance while she was in her encounter. Then when she got up off the floor, she was completely healed physically.

At this point, I would like to bring caution. When having encounters with the Lord, we don't want to boss Him around. I remember hearing someone sharing about her experience and how she was telling God to do this and that. Something just didn't feel right about bossing God around. Another thing is that we are not having this experience to conjure up dead people or angels. That would be necromancy, which is conjuring up the dead. It is a form of sorcery.

In First Samuel 28:1-15 (NKJV), we see what happened to Saul when he tried that:

> *Now it happened in those days that the Philistines gathered their armies together for war, to fight with Israel. And Achish said to David, "You assuredly know that you will go out with me to battle, you and your men."*
>
> *And David said to Achish, "Surely you know what your servant can do." And Achish said to David, "Therefore I will make you one of my chief guardians forever." Now Samuel had died, and all Israel had lamented for him and buried him in Ramah, in his own city. And Saul had put the mediums and the spiritists out of the land.*
>
> *Then the Philistines gathered together, and came and encamped at Shunem. So Saul gathered all Israel together, and they encamped at Gilboa.*
>
> *When Saul saw the army of the Philistines, he was afraid, and his heart trembled greatly. And when Saul inquired of the Lord, the Lord did not answer him, either by dreams or by Urim or by the prophets.*
>
> *Then Saul said to his servants, "Find me a woman who is a medium, that I may go to her and inquire of her." And his servants said to him, "In fact, there is a woman who is a medium at En Dor."*

So Saul disguised himself and put on other clothes, and he went, and two men with him; and they came to the woman by night. And he said, "Please conduct a séance for me, and bring up for me the one I shall name to you."

Then the woman said to him, "Look, you know what Saul has done, how he has cut off the mediums and the spiritists from the land. Why then do you lay a snare for my life, to cause me to die?"

And Saul swore to her by the Lord, saying, "As the Lord lives, no punishment shall come upon you for this thing."

Then the woman said, "Whom shall I bring up for you?" And he said, "Bring up Samuel for me."

When the woman saw Samuel, she cried out with a loud voice. And the woman spoke to Saul, saying, "Why have you deceived me? For you are Saul!"

And the king said to her, "Do not be afraid. What did you see?" And the woman said to Saul, "I saw a spirit ascending out of the earth."

So he said to her, "What is his form?" And she said, "An old man is coming up, and he is covered with a mantle." And Saul perceived that it was Samuel, and he stooped with his face to the ground and bowed down.

Now Samuel said to Saul, "Why have you disturbed me by bringing me up?"

The result was literally deadly for Saul and for his sons as well. Samuel told him in verse 19 that Israel would be handed over to the Philistines and that the next day he and his sons would die. This is nothing to mess with and something that God seems to feel pretty strongly about.

Several years after Bill's dad died, one of the women in our church was standing around before the service started one Sunday, and she was looking at the back door of the church watching the people come in. She did a double take because she saw Bill's dad walk in and walk around the room. She was not expecting that at all and was, to say the least, shocked. I think that when we least expect it, God splits the wall between the visible and the invisible, and we can have a peak at what is going on in the heavenly realm.

We should have no interest in making things like this happen. When they do, it's an exciting time, but we need to be careful not to cross that line and go astray.

One of my favorite stories in the Bible about this subject of heavenly encounters is that of John the beloved. In Revelation 4:1-3 (NKJV), John tells of his vision:

> *After these things I looked, and behold, a door standing open in heaven. And the first voice which I heard was like a trumpet speaking with me, saying, "Come up here, and I will show you things which must take place after this." Immediately I was in the Spirit; and behold, a throne set in heaven, and One sat on the throne. And He who sat there was like a jasper and a sardius stone in appearance; and there was a rainbow around the throne, in appearance like an emerald.*

This was one of many encounters that John had. After reading John's encounters, we can see that it is God's intention to take us into His realm to uncover His glorious mysteries.

So many of us have been crying out for more of Heaven to come to earth. I believe that God is answering our prayers and lifting that veil and letting us experience Him. The place between the invisible and the visible is becoming, as St. Patrick said, "thin."

As we pray, "Thy Kingdom come, Thy will be done on earth as it is in Heaven," know that He is answering our prayers because He loves us with an everlasting love. He wants all men and women and children to experience this love and be changed into His likeness.

CONCLUSION

At different times I have wondered if the visions would end, but they have continued. However, the visions are different and the lessons are harder for me to learn. I am finding that I have to stay in one place longer to understand the lesson God is teaching me. I have learned of God's delight in our different personalities, how we all have a different tone and song of our own. I have also learned how we are to recognize the presence of the Father, Son, and Holy Spirit at all times, and how to live above the forest. I have even jumped into a pool of brightness—and I'm wearing it like an ice cream cone dipped in chocolate coating.

I want you to know that my prayer for you is:

That He would grant you, according to the riches of His glory, to be strengthened with power through His

Holy Spirit in the inner man, so that Christ may dwell in your hearts through faith; and that you, being rooted and grounded in love, may be able to comprehend with all the saints what is the breadth and length and height and depth, and to know the love of Christ which passes knowledge, that you may be filled up to all the fullness of God (Ephesians 3:16-19).

Author Contact
Information

Judy's email contact for speaking:
judyfranklin@me.com

Beni's email contact for speaking:
prayfor5@aol.com

Bethel Church
933 College View Drive
Redding, CA 96003
www.ibethel.org

AUTHOR'S BOOK RECOMMENDATIONS

The Happy Intercessor
by Beni Johnson

Dreaming With God
by Bill Johnson

Discovering the Seer in You: Exploring Your Prophetic Gifts
by James Goll

*The Supernatural Ways of Royalty: Discovering Your Right
and Privileges of Being a Son or Daughter of God*
by Kris Vallotton and Bill Johnson

In the right hands, This Book will Change Lives!

Most of the people who need this message will not be looking for this book. To change their lives, you need to put a copy of this book in their hands.

> *But others (seeds) fell into good ground, and brought forth fruit, some a hundred-fold, some sixty-fold, some thirty-fold* (Matthew 13:8).

Our ministry is constantly seeking methods to find the good ground, the people who need this anointed message to change their lives. Will you help us reach these people?

> *Remember this—a farmer who plants only a few seeds will get a small crop. But the one who plants generously will get a generous crop* (2 Corinthians 9:6).

EXTEND THIS MINISTRY BY SOWING
3 BOOKS, 5 BOOKS, 10 BOOKS, **OR MORE TODAY,**
AND BECOME A LIFE CHANGER!

Thank you,

Don Nori Sr., Publisher
Destiny Image
Since 1982

DESTINY IMAGE PUBLISHERS, INC.

*"Speaking to the Purposes of God for This Generation
and for the Generations to Come."*

VISIT OUR NEW SITE HOME AT
WWW.DESTINYIMAGE.COM

FREE SUBSCRIPTION TO DI NEWSLETTER

Receive free unpublished articles by top DI authors, exclusive

discounts, and free downloads from our best and newest books.

Visit www.destinyimage.com to subscribe.

Write to: Destiny Image
               P.O. Box 310
               Shippensburg, PA 17257-0310

Call: 1-800-722-6774

Email: orders@destinyimage.com

For a complete list of our titles or to place an order
online, visit www.destinyimage.com.

FIND US ON FACEBOOK OR FOLLOW US ON TWITTER.

www.facebook.com/destinyimage   **facebook**
www.twitter.com/destinyimage   **twitter**